THE HAND-BOOK LIBRARY—NOS. 2-3.

ISSUED QUARTERLY.
SUBSCRIPTION PRICE, $1.00 PER YEAR.

MARCH, 1890.

Copyrighted, 1890, by Street & Smith.

Entered at the Post Office, New York, as Second-Class Matter.

TITLED AMERICANS.

A LIST OF

AMERICAN LADIES

WHO HAVE MARRIED FOREIGNERS OF RANK.

ANNUALLY REVISED.

ILLUSTRATED WITH ARMORIAL BEARINGS.

HERALDIC CROWN.

D1489122

INTRODUCTION

Bessie. Jennie, Lizzie. Mary, Nellie and Annie. There was something fairly ordinary in the names of these young American heiresses who had embarked upon the great adventure of a marriage into the European aristocracy. They suggested perhaps a graduating class of a high school in Connecticut or Ohio. But these are far from ordinary Americans, for their names appear in *Titled Americans*, an 1890 book that revealed the wealthiest and most socially ambitious families of late nineteenth-century America, and the titled European bachelors whose hearts their daughters might hope to conquer.

It has been estimated that 454 American heiresses married European aristocrats in the late nineteenth century, and thus acquired, at considerable expense, hereditary titles of nobility. 136 bagged Earls or Counts, forty-two married princes, seventeen married dukes, nineteen married viscounts, thirty-three married marquises, and there are forty-six wives of baronets and knights, and sixty-four baronesses. Scholars such as Maureen Montgomery and Marian Fowler have significantly enriched our understanding of the headhunting heiresses.

People were indeed curious about such fairy-tale marriages. In the last two or three decades of the nineteenth century, there had been an explosion of press interest in the doings of the wealthy, who – led by the regal Astors, Vanderbilts, Morgans and Goulds – became objects of intense press scrutiny. The rich constituted the first true celebrities in American life, soon to be followed by opera divas, Broadway performers, singers, movie stars, professional athletes, gamblers and gangsters. Celebrity was an elastic category in America, and the aspiration to be a celebrity swept across the nation in the late nineteenth century. Parties given at the highest levels of society were described in the press. The summer 'cottages' at Newport (which were really quite handsome French Renaissance country estates) were photographed, and praised in lavish, sycophantic detail. Tourists headed for Fifth Avenue and Newport, hoping for a sight of the celebrity hostesses and heiresses of the day. There was newly created space for 'society news' in many major American newspapers. In an era of increasing journalistic specialization, there were newly hired columnists and reporters devoted to high society.

Publishers were quick to notice this development in the journalistic marketplace. An explosion of guides to the way of life of the *bon ton*, lists of the fashionables and ultra-fashionables, and guides which sought to rank the richest men, the most exclusive gentlemen's clubs, and the most eligible bachelors and society belles soon followed.

Among the earliest ventures was *The List*, a directory of social information published by Maurice M. Minton in 1880, aimed at the several thousand families who made up society in New York City. It was followed by Charles H. Crandall's *The Season: An Annual Record of Society in New York, Brooklyn, and Vicinity* (1883). The viperish society gossip weekly magazine, *Town Topics*, began its notorious career in 1885. The most influential and long-lived guide to those at the highest social standing was *The Social Register* (appearing annually from 1887). But it was a remark by the social arbiter Ward McAlister which set the seal upon the idea of aristocratic New York city. 'Why,' he remarked to a journalist, 'there are only about four hundred people in fashionable New York society.' Across the nation there was an outcry. Who were the 400? Who was excluded?

The 1890s was a decade in which social conflict reached unprecedented heights, and hardship was a reality for many Americans. Consciences were agitated by the documentation of the lives of the New York slum-dwellers in Jacob Riis' *How The Other Half Lives*, published in 1890. But newspapers in what was called the Gilded Age seemed to be more concerned to chronicle the lives of the rich and socially eminent. The idea of McAllister's 400 in the 1890s seemed a more interesting social phenomenon. *Titled Americans* emerged out of that swirling curiosity about the social elite.

Novelists of the distinction of Henry James and Edith Wharton found in the social aspirations of American womanhood, and the reality of their encounter with European aristocrats, a subject of potential tragedy. But the nuanced portraiture of *The Portrait of a Lady* or *The House of Mirth* scarcely shaped the avid interest of the majority of novel-readers or the target audience for daily papers. The interest was unquenched, and largely uncritical.

The most astringent view of these golden marriages came from those who assumed that there were financial transactions and substantial dowries behind them. *The New York Times* suggested in 1893 that as much as $50 million might have accompanied the American brides as they sailed across the Atlantic for their new lives in the decayed and impoverished estates of the great aristocratic families. In 1911 Gustavus Myers estimated the true cost of the transatlantic marriages at something like $220 million.

The problem with putting a figure, a very large figure, to the transatlantic marriages is that it over-simplifies what was a complex process. Marriage into European noble families was not something to be settled by hauling out a cheque book and buying a husband for Bessie. Jennie, Lizzie. Mary, Nellie or Annie.

Consider the case of Lily Hamersley and Jennie Jerome, New York heiresses who became sisters-in-law by marrying into the Marlborough family. Jerome, who married Lord Randolph Churchill, third son of the 7th Duke, in 1874, appears in *Titled Americans*. Hamersley, who married Lord Randolph's older brother, George Spencer-Churchill, 8th Duke of Marlborough, in 1888, is mentioned in the Preface. Their situations were intriguingly similar. Lord Randolph Churchill's biographer, R.F. Foster, found evidence that Francis Knollys, a family friend and equerry to the Prince of Wales, compiled detailed reports on the state of the Jerome finances. It was reported in the New York press that the 8th Duke ordered that 'a strict and searching investigation into Mrs. Hamersley's pecuniary eligibility' should be undertaken. The Jerome family had doubts about Lord Randolph. He was regarded by Jerome's mother as a disaster waiting to happen: he was 'hasty... rash... headstrong... unconsidered... impulsive.' Lily Hamersley, a worldly and quick-witted widow of a wealthy New York real estate mogul, looked no less closely into the 8th Duke's finances and reputation. That he was divorced, and that his ex-wife was still living, raised no end of problems within the Anglican and Episcopalian communities. There was also an illegitimate son, and his having been named as a co-respondent in the 1886 divorce trial of Lady Colin Campbell.

And when everything was settled, it was time to bring in the lawyers for a careful consideration of the settlement, especially taking into account the different legal frameworks which applied to the property of married women in the United States (where a bride retained her property and wealth) and Great Britain (where husbands assumed unrestricted control over the wealth and property of the women they married). Running through the first series of Julian Fellowes' Downton Abbey, first aired on British television in 2010, was the dire consequences for the heiress played by Elizabeth McGovern when she married the Earl of Grantham. On their marriage her great fortune was incorporated into the comital entail, in perpetuity. A wise heiress, and her parents and lawyers, would need to know about the perils of such a marriage. There was indeed much to negotiate. And when the families' objections seemed interminable, it was sometimes necessary to force their hands. Winston Churchill was born seven months after the wedding of Jennie Jerome and Lord Randolph Churchill. The 7th Duke and the Duchess were not reconciled, and declined to attend the wedding.

Jerome and Lord Randolph were married at the British Embassy in Paris. Hamersley and the 8th Duke were married by the Mayor of New York in City Hall. Another ill-fated

New York heiress to marry into the Marlborough family was Consuelo Vanderbilt, daughter of William Kissam Vanderbilt, railroad magnate. The marriage settlement in 1895 benefited the 9th Duke of Marlborough by some $2.5 million in railroad stock. (They separated in 1906, and were formally divorced in 1921.)

Behind the simple lists of aristocratic marriages in *Titled Americans* there is a world of complexity, scandal, family problems and financial and legal concerns. There was sufficient drama in such marriages to keep society gossips happy. And when the time came for divorce or widowhood, the merry-go-round of gossip and press attention resumed.

No author's name appears on the title page of *Titled Americans*, but we may fill in the details of authorship, which was a story as interesting as some of those on his list. It was written (or, more accurately, compiled) by a husband and wife team of minor European aristocrats who came to the United States on the rebound from a marital financial crisis.[1]

They were snobs on the make, as one might assume, who traded on their supposed insider status as aristocrats in the American journalistic and publishing market, which was increasingly fascinated by things aristocratic. When all

[1] The title-page of the 1890 *Titled Americans* is reproduced on http://edwardianpromenade.com/women/titled-americans-giveaway/ (seen 5 March 2013), with a hand-annotation: 'Compiled by Philip Frederick Cunliffe-Owen.' His wife's participation is an appropriate surmise. Reporting her estate on January 18, 1930, *The New York Times* noted their collaborative work: 'No value was found for a mass of newspaper clippings, dealing mainly with the foreign aristocracy, upon which the Cunliffe-Owens relied to a large extent in writing articles.'

bequests were made, the estate of Marguerite Cunliffe-Owen, widow of the former diplomat Frederick Cunliffe-Owen, amounted to $8,338. It was left to Dr. Edward F. Sutton, Mrs. Cunliffe-Owen's long-term chauffeur. *The New York Times* reported that when her possessions were sold at auction in 1828, the most valuable piece went for $150. We are not talking here about a couple who lived the life of the aristocracy about which they seemed to possess such striking inside knowledge, but a couple of hustlers, largely down on their luck.

Frederick Cunliffe-Owen, CBE (1854 -1926) was the son of a Cheshire baronet with a string of honours after his name (K.C.B, K.C.M.G). His mother was Jenny, Baroness von Reitzenstein, from an aristocratic German family much noticed in the *Almanach de Gotha*. He was educated at a reputable public school (Lancing) and the University of Lausanne, before entering the diplomatic service. His work took him to Egypt and Japan.

Forced to resign from the diplomatic service when he encountered financial difficulties (no details are known), Cunliffe-Owen emigrated to the United States in 1885, where he launched a career in New York as a commentator on international relations, writing as 'Ex-Attaché' and 'Veteran Diplomat.' He also was a contributor to *The New York Times*, writing unsigned editorials on diplomacy and foreign affairs and society columns, and was believed to have been affiliated in some capacity with the New York Tribune, under the proprietorship of Whitelaw Reid. An avid collector of European honours, Cunliffe-Owen became Grand Officer of the Crown of Italy, the Order of

Knighthood of Orange-Nassau in the Netherlands, and received the White Eagle of Serbia. In New York he became a noted clubman. He seemed to be the classic insider, the man who knew everyone who mattered.

His wife Marguerite, daughter of Count Jules du Planty, was an historical novelist and biographer who wrote widely under the pseudonym 'La Marquise de Fontenoy.' She specialized in accounts of the social life of the royal courts of Europe. (Her true identity only became known later.) Her books were rich in secrets, hints of scandal. The tone for her literary career is suggested by the full title of *Within Royal Palaces*, published in 1892, *A Brilliant and Charmingly Written Inner Life View of Emperors, Kings, Queens, Princes, and Princesses . . . Written from a Personal Knowledge of Scenes Behind the Thrones, by the Marquise de Fontenoy*. Between 1899 and 1910, La Marquise published one book after another, each promising sensational revelations about court life.

Her style, modeled after the tone of Col. Mann's *Town Topics*, was to insinuate scandal, and then vigorously offer a denial and vindication. 'The legitimacy of the birth of both the present and the late King of Spain,' she wrote in 1902, 'has been called into question. Of course, it is only political prejudice of the basest order that could have mustered up a sufficient amount of venom to impugn the virtue of that most estimable woman, the present Queen Regent Christina.'

Together, the Cunliffe-Owens put together *Titled Americans* for publication 1890. It may have been planned as an annual publication, to be revised and reissued as demand suggested. But the only further revision appeared twenty-five years later, in 1915, compiled by Arthur E. Hartzell (1891-1940), a journalist on the 'War Desk' of *The New York Times*. Hartzell volunteered for the Army in 1917, and was promoted to Captain on the staff of General Pershing's headquarters of the American Expeditionary Force. His skills as a journalist and wordsmith were put to use in his account of the Meuse-Argonne battle, September 26 – November 11, 1918, designed for the use of press correspondents. Hartzell worked for the J. Walter Thompson advertising agency after the war. His career took him far from the world of the Cunliffe-Owens.

The war turned American attention away from the heiresses, and did much to destroy the world of the European aristocracy. It was Hollywood, not aristocratic chateaux in Europe, which caught the imagination of Americans in the interwar years. But the Cunliffe-Owens left their stamp upon the project. *Titled Americans* belonged to a time when innocent social climbing fascinated the American public. With the entry into the European war in 1917, the enthusiasm on Fifth Avenue in New York for crests and coats of arms, for private yachts and servants in livery, so strong throughout the 1890s and resurrected in the 1920s, was seen with different eyes. The mansion rented by Jay Gatsby in Scott Fitzgerald's *The Great Gatsby* (1925), located on the north shore of Long Island, belonged to the new postwar world of easy money and celebrity. Attending his first party at Gatsby's mansion, the narrator, Nick Carraway, noted a number of well-dressed young Englishmen, 'all looking a little hungry, and all talking in low, earnest voices to solid and prosperous Americans. I was sure that they were selling something: bonds or insurance or automobiles.' On the surface it might appear to be a world unknown to the Cunliffe-Owens, but they, too, were in the marketplace, offering an impressive line in heiresses and eligible aristocrats. In the pages of *Titled Americans* they may have put their finger upon one of those quietly interesting truths about American life in the 1890s, that the democratic and egalitarian spirit was thinner than most supposed.

Eric Homberger
Emeritus Professor of American Studies,
University of East Anglia, Norwich

Suggested Further Reading

Fowler, Marian. *In a Gilded Cage: From Heiress to Duchess.* Random House of Canada, 1993.
Hartzell, A.E. (compiler). *Titled Americans,* 1915.
'Have Found Husbands Abroad,' *New York Times,* April 19, 1893.
Homberger, Eric, Mrs Astor's New York: *Money and Social Power in a Gilded Age.* Yale University Press, 2002.
'How You May Join the 400: Ward McAllister Tells the Long-Sought Secret,' *New York World,* October 18, 1891.
McAllister, Ward. *Society as I Have Found It.* Cassell Publishing, 1890.

INTRODUCTION

Martin, Ralph G. *Jennie: The Life of Lady Randolph Churchill: The Romantic Years 1854–1895*. Prentice Hall, 1969.

Montgomery, Maureen. *Gilded Prostitution: Status, Money and Transatlantic Marriages, 1870-1914*. Routledge, 1989.

Myers, Gustavus. *History of the Great American Fortunes*. Charles H. Kerr, 1911.

Nicholls, C.W. de Lyon. *The 469 Ultra-Fashionables of America*. Broadway Pub. Co, 1912.

'Origin of the "Four Hundred",' *Valentine's Manual of Old New York*, I (1916), 63-65.

Patterson, Jerry E. *Fifth Avenue: The Best Address*. Rizzoli, 1998.

Patterson, Jerry E. *The First Four Hundred: Mrs. Astor's New York in the Gilded Age*. Rizzoli, 2000.

Riis, Jacob. How *The Other Half Lives*. Charles Scribner's Sons, 1890.

Stuart, Amanda Mackenzie. *Consuelo and Alva Vanderbilt: The Story of a Daughter and a Mother in the Gilded Age*. Harper Collins, 2005.

Svenson, Sally E. *Lily, Duchess of Marlborough (1854 – 1909): A Portrait with Husbands*. Dog Ear Publishing, 2011.

The 400 (*Officially Supervised*), 1890.

CONTENTS.

	PAGE.
Abbott, Miss Ellen F.	48
Allen, Miss	109
Andrews, Miss Isabella	86
Appleton, Miss Alice	80
Austin, Miss Emmeline	85
Bachmann, Miss Elise	102
Bartlett, Miss (Senora Oviedo)	67
Beale, Miss Mary	34
Beauvar-Boosier, Miss Marie Adele B.	103
Benham, Miss Ada	63
Berdan, Miss	84
Binney, Miss Mary	31
Blake, Miss Mary	53
Blunt, Miss Anna	105
Broadwood, Miss Eva	109
Burn, Miss Eliza Jane	68
Butterfield, Miss	93
Carey, Miss Elizabeth	117
Carroll, Miss	79
Carroll, Miss Agnes	78
Carroll, Miss E.	71
Carroll, Miss Sarah Virginia (Mrs. Charles Griffin)	62
Chamberlain, Miss Jennie	86
Chisholm, Miss.	83
Christ, Miss (Mrs. Berna)	98
Christmas, Miss Norma	33
Chizelle, Miss Elizabeth	116
Claffin, Miss Jennie	55
Conrad, Miss	118
Corbin, Miss Elizabeth	92
Corbin, Miss Louise	125
Corbin, Miss Mary	58
Curtis, Miss Bessie	117

3

CONTENTS.—(Continued.)

	PAGE.
Curtis, Miss Josephine Mary	108
Dahlgren, Miss	99
Dana, Miss	96
Davis, Miss Mathilde	82
Day, Miss	81
Donohue, Miss	114
Dubarry, Mrs. Col. Frank (Mrs. Wm. G. Chandler)	104
Dunlap, Miss Margaret	42
Endicott, Miss Mary	49
Field, Miss	116
Field, Miss Elizabeth Hickson	42
Field, Miss Jeanie Lucinda	94
Fish, Miss Edith Livingston	97
Fisher, Miss	67
Fisher, Miss Blanche	34
Fisher, Miss Mary	29
Forbes, Miss Mary Elizabeth	106
Forster, Miss Anna	115
Friedner, Miss Louise	122
Frost, Miss Evelyn	37
Frost, Miss Jane G.	91
Frost, Miss Louise	120
Fry, Miss	118
Gallatin, Mrs. Herbert	49
Garrison, Miss Estelle	108
Gillender, Miss	110
Gilmour, Miss Eliza	90
Goddard, Miss Catherine Maud Elis	102
Gordon, Miss Emily	124
Grant, Miss Mary	52
Grant, Miss Nellie	111
Gratiot, Miss Mary	93
Greenough, Miss (Mrs Charles Moulton)	87
Greene, Miss Georgiana Frances	31
Greene, Miss Josephine	126
Haight, Miss	120
Hamilton, Miss Margaret	127
Hammond, Miss Mary	83
Hatcher, Miss Louise	69
Hensler, Miss Elise	61
Heyward, Miss Mary	51

4

CONTENTS. – (Continued.)

PAGE.

Hoffmann, Miss Medorah Marie..................................... 93
Holman, Miss.. 92
Hooper, Miss Mary.. 29
Hoyt, Miss Susan G... 65
Hungerford, Miss Ada... 118
Hutton, Miss Annie... 91
Hutton, Miss Fannie.. 101
Jansen, Miss Marie... 92
Jay, Miss.. 113
Jones, Miss.. 94
Jones, Miss Maria Ida.. 110
Jones, Miss Mary... 119
Jerome, Miss... 66
Jerome, Miss Jennie.. 53
Jerome, Miss Leonie Blanche.. 84
King, Miss... 124
King, Miss Mary.. 125
King, Miss Mary Livingstone.. 32
Kinney, Miss Constance... 67
Kirby, Miss Mary... 63
Lawrence, Miss Frances Margaret.................................... 121
Lee, Miss Lucy Tracy... 59
Lee, Miss Mary Esther (Princess Frederick)......................... 126
Ledoux, Miss Anita... 46
Ledoux, Miss Mary.. 120
Lewis, Miss Mary... 30
Livingston, Miss Elizabeth... 38
Lorillard, Mrs. George L... 48
Lothrop, Miss Emily.. 76
Lousay, Miss Mary.. 80
Low, Miss Jessie... 69
Luckers, Miss Ella... 36
Mackay, Miss Eva Julia Bryant...................................... 54
Magruder, Miss Helen... 28
McAllister, Miss... 122
McCall, Miss Meta.. 60
McCarthy, Miss Amelie.. 64
McKeene, Miss.. 127
McKnight, Miss Caroline.. 44
McLaw, Miss Helen.. 46
McLean, Miss Jessie.. 56

CONTENTS.—(Continued.)

	PAGE.
McVicker, Miss Katherine	70
Meiggs, Miss	97
Meinell, Miss Arnalie	80
Meinell, Miss Elizabeth	83
Meinell, Miss Mary	34
Miltenberger, Miss	106
Minturn, Miss Susan Carter	35
Montgomery, Miss Eulalie	39
Montgomery, Miss Laura	105
Moore, Miss Mary	40
Morgan, Miss May Tevis	101
Motley, Miss Elizabeth (Mrs. J. P. Ives)	71
Motley, Miss Mary L	115
Motley, Miss Susan	90
Moulton, Miss Helen	76
Moulton, Miss Mary	103
Murphy, Miss Anita Theresa	128
Murphy, Miss Matilda Josephine	43
Niven, Miss Mary	114
O'Donnell, Miss Alice	82
Orne, Miss Katherine	37
O'Sullivan, Miss Emily	107
Page, Miss Elizabeth T. (Mrs. T. Bispham)	41
Palmer, Miss Juliette	30
Parker, Miss Mary Elizabeth (Mrs. J. P. Bouligny)	85
Parkes, Miss Kate	94
Parrott, Miss Isabelle	59
Parsons, Miss May	87
Penniman, Miss Helen	38
Peters, Miss Sidonie	39
Phalen, Miss Catherine	95
Phalen, Miss Florence	68
Pilie, Miss	52
Pilie, Miss Marie	74
Plummer, Miss Mary	55
Polk, Miss Mary	50
Porter, Miss Ella	48
Pourtales, Countess Bertha	104
Price, Miss Lilian (Mrs. Louis Hamersley)	89
Ray, Miss	57
Reade, Miss Mary	64

CONTENTS. – (Continued.)

PAGE.

Reid, Miss Ann... 33
Richardson, Miss Martha Ellen................................. 78
Ridgeway, Miss.. 66
Riggs, Miss Cecilia.. 75
Roberts, Miss Emily Augusta................................... 73
Roosevelt, Miss Cornelia...................................... 113
Russell, Miss Edith.. 100
Sampson, Miss Adele.. 60
Sanger, Miss Helen... 95
Schaumberg, Miss Emily.. 73
Schenck, Miss Mary... 121
Sharon, Miss Florence Emily................................... 77
Shenley, Miss Elizabeth....................................... 72
Sibley, Miss Jane.. 81
Singer, Mrs. Isaac... 46
Singer, Miss Isabella.. 58
Singer, Miss Winnaretta...................................... 112
Slidell, Miss.. 62
Slidell, Miss.. 116
Slocomb, Miss Cora... 43
Smith, Miss Mary Whiteall..................................... 56
Smith, Miss Mimi... 65
Stager, Miss Ellen... 45
Stevens, Miss Mary... 99
Stokes, Miss... 114
Story, Miss Mary... 98
Spencer, Miss Eleanor.. 123
Terry, Miss.. 41
Thomas, Miss Helen... 32
Thornburgh, Miss Virginia S................................... 57
Thorndike, Miss Ella... 111
Thorne, Miss... 65
Thorne, Miss... 100
Traer, Miss Helen Rebecca.................................... 122
Urquhardt, Miss Amelie....................................... 36
Van Auken, Miss Jessie....................................... 119
Wadsworth, Miss Cornelia...................................... 29
Wadsworth, Miss Mary (Mrs. Arthur Post)....................... 112
Walker, Miss Mary.. 50
Ward, Miss Adele A... 44
Warden, Miss Juliet.. 47

CONTENTS.—(Continued.)

	PAGE.
Wheelright, Miss	66
Wickershaw, Miss	77
Wickershaw, Miss	119
Williams, Miss Harriet	40
Willing, Miss Annie	96
Wilson, Miss Belle	74
Work, Miss Frances	107
Yznaga del Valle, Miss Consuela	88
Yznaga del Valle, Miss Natica	79
Zerega, Miss Lizzie	51
The Royal Family	129 to 155
A Carefully Compiled List of Peers who are supposed to be eager to lay their Coronets, and incidentally their Hearts, at the feet of the all-conquering American Girl	156 to 193
The Great Ball of 1890	194 to 252
Why English Noblemen Seek American Brides—Chauncey M. Depew's Views on the Subject	253 to 258

John Watts de Peyster, LL. D.

1887.

Master of Arts, Columbia College of New York, 1872.—Hon. Mem. Clarendon Hist. Soc., Edinburgh, Scotland ; of the New Brunswick Hist. Soc., St. John, Canada ; of the Hist. Soc. of Minnesota, Montana, New Jersey ; of the Military Order of the Loyal Legion of the U. S., &c.; of the N. Y. Burns' Club, &c.; Cor. Mem. of the Quebec Lit. and Hist. Soc., Canada, &c. ; Life Mem. Royal Hist. Soc. of Great Britain, London, Eng. ; Mem. Maatschappij Nederlandsche Letterkunde, Leyden, Holland.—First Hon. Mem. Third Army Corps (A. of the P.) Union ; Hon. Mem. Third Army Corps Gettysburg Battlefield Reunion and Mem. of the Honorary Committee ; Mem. Amer. Hist. Association, U. S. A. ; of the Holland Society, N. Y. ; Associate Mem. Military Institution of the U. S., &c., &c. ; Member, Life, Honorary and Corresponding Member of over forty State and Local Historical, Scientific and Literary Societies and Associations, &c., at home and abroad.—Colonel N. Y. S. I., 1846, assigned for "meritorious conduct" to command of 22d Regimental District, M. F. S. N. Y., 1849 ; Brig.-General for "important service" [first appointment in N. Y. State to that rank, hitherto elective], 1851, M. F. S. N. Y. ; Military Agent S. N. Y., in Europe, 1851-53, authorized and endorsed by U. S. A., 1851-3 ; assisted in organization of present Police, N. Y., and first reported in favor of Paid Fire Department with Fire Escapes and Steam Engines, 1852-3 ; Adjutant-General S. N. Y., 1855 ; Brevet Major-General S. N. Y. for "meritorious services," by "Special Act" or "Concurrent Resolution," N. Y. State Legislature, April, 1866, [first and only General officer receiving such an honor (the highest) from S. N. Y., and the only officer *thus* brevetted (Major-General) in the United States].

PREFACE.

The increasing frequency of marriages between American ladies, and foreigners possessed of either official or social rank in Europe, and the absence of any complete list and record of such matrimonial alliances, renders the publication of "Titled Americans" desirable, and even necessary as a work of reference.

When Mrs. Louis Hamersley became the wife of the Duke of Marlborough, in July, 1888, she was described at the time by the newspapers as the "American Duchess," and the impression was conveyed to, and accepted by the public, that she was the only American lady entitled to ducal rank. The latter, however, is far from being the case. For there are no less than ten or twelve Duchesses now living who are of American parentage and birth. Two or three of them have been married for more than a quarter of a century, and have become so separated in interests, obligations, and environments from the land of their birth, that they have been forgotten, and allowed to pass out of remembrance of the present generation in the United States.

Besides the ten or twelve American girls who

have married European Dukes, there are nearly twenty who have contracted alliances with Princes, while about the same number are wedded to foreign ambassadors at the various courts of Europe. In Rome alone the Swedish, the Danish, and the Dutch ministers plenipotentiary have each of them American wives, while at St. Petersburg the German and the Wurtemberg Ambassadresses are both of good old New York stock.

Exception may possibly be taken to the name of "Titled Americans," on the ground that this work deals exclusively with American ladies who have married foreigners of rank, and that all reference to American men who have received honors or distinctions from European sovereigns or governments has been omitted. Mr. John Buck, of San Francisco, Mr. Loubar, of New York, Mr. Good, of Brooklyn, and several other well-known citizens of the United States, have been created Count by the Pope, while Mr. Murphy, of the San Francisco dry-goods firm of Murphy, Grant & Co., and Mr. D. J. Oliver, derive their titles of Marquis from the same source. These honorific distinctions are, however, not officially recognized in this country, and their use is not in accordance with the democratic institutions and social system of the United States. To such an extent is this the case, that when an alien is admitted under the naturalization laws to the rights of American

citizenship, he is forced by sections 2,165–74 of
the revised statutes of the United States, to make
" an express renunciation of any hereditary title
or order of nobility" which he may have borne
until that time.

Exception may also be taken to the fact that a
certain number of ladies who figure in this work
appear without " handles to their names." It
must, however, be borne in mind that the junior
branches of English noble families do not bear
titles, and that the untitled country families or
gentry authorized by government to the use of
coat armor, are regarded both at home and abroad
as constituting the backbone of the British aristocracy. Indeed an untitled County Esquire of
ancient lineage, enjoys far higher consideration
than the bearer of a title of relatively recent creation. The right to bear coats of arms, not of
titles, has ever been considered the distinctive
mark of the true noblesse.

Special pains have been taken to prevent the
insertion in this work of names which are not
strictly entitled to figure therein. All titles have
been omitted concerning the origin and authentic-
ity of which the slightest doubt prevails, and the
only persons who appear in the pages of " Titled
Americans" are those whose names are recorded
in the jealously guarded Libri d' Oro of the various
governments of Europe.

INTRODUCTION.

Nobiliary titles do not necessarily confer what is strictly known as nobility or noblesse upon their bearers. Paradoxical though it may appear there are quite a large number of Barons, Counts, Marquises, Princes, and even Dukes, who do not belong to the nobility, and who possess none of the few remaining privileges which have been retained by that favored class in the monarchical countries of Europe; while on the other hand there are many gentlemen—the French term of "gentilhomme" would be their more correct designation—who, although untitled, enjoy a precedence and a consideration which no mere peerage could confer. King James I., of Great Britain, who was singularly shrewd in certain things, used frequently to remark that "the sovereign, though he can make a noble, cannot make a gentleman." The gentry or gentilhommerie and the nobility or noblesse are one and the same thing. Whether titled or not they form a class apart. Their privileged position is due to their lineage, and to the right which they have inherited of bearing coat armor. It is the duly legalized bearing of heraldic arms, not of titles, which is everywhere in Europe considered as the distinctive mark of the true noblesse. Mere titles can be conferred by the more or less merited favor of any monarch great or small. But no Emperor, however powerful, can confer lineage ancestry and the consideration which is attached thereto. Hence it happens that while on the one hand there are Dukes and Princes who are not regarded as " hoffahig " that is admissible to court, there are on the other hand many untitled gentilhommes whose birth and lineage render them " Tafel-fahig " and fit to associate with imperial and royal personages on terms of intimacy which may almost be described as equality. " Tafelfahig " is a German court expression, used to designate persons whose pedigree is of sufficient length and purity to render them worthy of sitting at the royal table on State occasions. During the past four decades, titles have been granted with the most reckless profusion—in many cases for mere financial assistance, rendered not to the State, but to the personal treasury of some member of the reigning family. To such an extent has this been the case, that in Spain, Italy and Portugal, the members of the really ancient families avoid using their titles when among their equals in birth and merely designate one another by the prefix of " Don" or " Dona." Thus in Roman society no one would ever dream of alluding to Mrs. "Bonanza" Mackay's son-in-law as the Prince of Ralatro-Colonna, but merely as Don Ferdinand Colonna, while at Madrid the Duchess of Medina—Coeli, is invariably addressed as Dona Angela. The most punctilious use, however, of the title is made by these aristocrats in addressing any peer of recent creation, and the stress laid by them on the word "Duke," "Marquis," or "Count," on such occasions is more pointed than polite.

Having thus attempted to define what the Austrian Prime Minister Count Taaffe meant to say when he cynically observed the other day that "there are nobles and nobles," I will now venture to briefly describe the relative value of the various titles in each of the great European States.

RUSSIA.

There is in reality no aristocracy in Russia. It is true that there is a certain group of families which cluster round the court, and form the highest ranks of the " noblesse;" this social aristocracy contains many old families, but its real basis is mere official rank; it is of a semi-bureaucratic character, and the custom of dividing all landed property in equal shares among the children at the death of their parents deprives it of stability.

New men force their way into it by official distinction, while many of the old families are com-
pelled by sheer poverty to retire from its ranks.
The son of an humble village priest may rise to
the highest offices of State, while the descendants
of the Great Rurik may sink to the rank of peas-
ant. Titles possess even less value in Russia
than in the rest of Europe; they are very com-
mon, because the titled families are numerous,
and all the children bear the titles of their
parents, even during the parents' life. There are
hundreds, nay even thousands, of so-called Princes
and Princesses who have not the right to appear
at court, and who would not be admitted into the
society of St. Petersburg or of any other capital
of Europe. There is a Prince Krapotkine who is
earning his living as a cabman on the Newsky
Prospect; there is a Princess Galitzin who figures
in tights and spangles as a bareback rider in a
fourth-rate circus, and there is a member of the
Princely House of Eristoff de Gourie who has
served terms of penal servitude in several of the
convict prisons of Europe. Strictly speaking
their title of Prince is due to a misapprehension
and wrong translation. The Russian word used
to designate them is " Knyaz," the correct English synonym for which is " Lord." A " Knyaz,"
in fact, possesses much the same rank and position as an ordinary English Country Squire or

Lord of the Manor. During the reign of Louis XX. of France, two of these " Knyaz " happened to visit Versailles, and on inquiries being made by court officials concerning their rank, their interpreters, partly with a view of increasing their own importance, and partly through ignorance, translated the word " Knyaz " as Prince. Since then every Russian " squireen " has invariably been treated to the title of Prince from the very moment that he crossed the Czars' western frontier, much the same as every well-to-do Bombay peddler is greeted as a Rajah as soon as ever he sets foot in Paris. The titles of Count, and even of Baron, therefore enjoy far higher consideration in Russia than that of Prince. Since the days of Peter the Great there have been only sixty-seven creations of Count, and ten of that of Baron. Besides these there are a certain number of German Counts and Barons in the Baltic Provinces who are subjects of the Czar.

PORTUGAL.

Hereditary titles were abolished by the late King Louis, twenty years ago, in deference to popular sentiment on the subject, and all peerages and titular distinction, are held merely for life by their present possessors. They are not held in high estimation, either at home or abroad, on account of the singular ease with which they are obtained. Thus quite a number of English and French merchants engaged in the Portuguese trade have been able to obtain titles of Count, Viscount, and Baron, which in some cases they have subsequently proceeded to drag through the mud.

SPAIN.

In Spain titles abound to such an extent that they enjoy but little consideration, either at home or abroad. There are no less than 100 Dukes, 900 Marquesses, 800 Counts, 100 Viscounts, and about fifty Barons. There is an ex-hatter who is a Duke, and an ex-pedicure who has become a Count. In case of male issue, the titles pass down from father to eldest son; but in default thereof they are inherited by the eldest daughters who possess the singular privilege of transferring them to their husbands.

Thus A. M. Rosales, who was fortunate enough to capture the heart and hand of the heiress of the ducal house of Almodovar del Valle, has become Duke by his marriage. In the same manner Don Manuel Falcos has become, through his wife, Duke of Fernan-Nunez. Nobles who have thus obtained their titles by marriage are popularly known as " Duquesos," " Marquesos," and " Condesos."

Their children, while inheriting the mother's title, retain the father's patronymic, and thus it happens that while many of the ancient titles created by Charles V. and Philip II. still remain, they are held by families entirely distinct from the ones on which they were originally conferred. Thus the dukedom of Medina-Sidonia created by Charles V. and granted to the Guzman family, is now held by the noble house of Toledo, while the duchy of Albuquerque formerly owned by the Cueras to-day belongs to the Osorios. Two titles alone have been maintained in the male line direct, namely, the dukedoms of Osuna and Astorga. With the exception of about thirty titles granted in the sixteenth century, almost the entire number of Spanish peerages have been created during the present century.

In addition to these there is the " Grandezza," which carries with it " Hoffahigkeit," and " a number of court privileges," including that of remaining covered in the presence of the sovereign. There are but 300 Grandees and as a long line of ancestry is required on the part of the applicants for the honor it is a dignity exceedingly highly prized. It was first instituted by Charles V. in the year 1520, on his return from Germany after being crowned Emperor. Wishing to imitate Charlemagne, he created twelve Grandees or Peers.

The ceremony of conferring the Grandezza is extremely quaint and curious, and is described as an "Almohada," which literally translated means the taking possession of the cushion. The Grandezza does not in itself confer any title.

ITALY.

There are more titles in Italy than in any other country of Europe. This is due to the fact that up to the year 1859 every petty sovereign, and even certain cities and towns, possessed the privilege of conferring titles. At the present time not only the King, but also the Popes, distribute Dukedoms, Marquisates, and Countships with a most profuse liberality. Indeed it is a well-known fact that any person who has no criminal record standing against his name, and who is ready to pay what are termed the " droits de chacellerie," otherwise " Chancellor's dues," experiences no difficulty in securing the title which he desires. The dues for a creation of Count amount to $5,000, the difference between the Vatican and the Quirinal being that whereas the one exacts payment in gold, the other is content to receive it in paper money. The fees for a Dukedom amount to about $16,000. It is noteworthy that many of the Hebrew financiers and brokers throughout Europe are indebted for their titles to the Pope. These honors are hereditary, and are enjoyed by the children even during the life-time of their parents. This mushroom aristocracy must not, however, be confounded with the haughty old nobility of Rome, Turin, and Milan, who pride themselves on their exclusiveness and on the purity of their descent. There is absolutely no communication or intercourse between such families as the Orsini, the Colonna, and the Barberini, and the nobility of recent creation.

GERMANY AND AUSTRIA.

In Germany and Austro-Hungary the aristocracy has more than anywhere else retained its ancient privileges and rights. These, however, are of a more social than political nature. The higher ranks of official life and the great offices of the State are monopolized by the nobility. No person who does not possess a pedigree of a certain length can obtain any post at court. With but few exceptions the titles are borne by all the children even during the life-time of their parents. The law of primogeniture, however, prevails with regard to the family estates, which are generally entailed. The German and Austro-Hungarian aristocracy consists of Dukes, Princes, Markgraafs, Counts, Barons, Ritters, and Edlers, or merely nobles. A number of the Dukes and Princes are what is known as mediatised, that is to say deprived in 1806 and 1815 of the petty sovereignties which they had previously possessed. They were allowed to retain certain privileges including exemption from personal taxes, from duty as jurors, and from obligatory service in the army. Since the days of the great Metternich a large number of financiers have been created Barons and Ritters. Indeed hardly a single loan has been contracted by any German State without the leading bankers and brokers connected therewith receiving some hereditary nobiliary distinction. They, however, form a class apart, are known as the " Finanze-Adel," or nobility of finance, and are kept at an immense distance by the old aristocracy. The only people of their rank who consent to have some social dealings with them are the bureaucrats and government officials, who have attained their title after long years of service under government.

FRANCE.

In France titles at the present moment are somewhat at a discount. While on the one hand there are the representatives of those grand old

families, which formerly constituted the very
kernel of European " noblesse," there are on the
other hand thousands of persons who have, without the slightest authority, adopted titles and
names to which they have no right. It is true
that there is a law in France which ordains that
no one shall adopt a nobiliary title or even adorn
his button-hole with a foreign order without having previously obtained a permit in due form to do
so from the Grande Chancellerie of the Order of
the Legion of Honor; and infraction of the ordi-
nance is punishable by both fine and imprison-
ment. But since the overthrow of the empire and
the abolition of monarchy in France, no steps have
been taken by the government to enforce the law,
and people ornament their names with any titles
which suit their fancy. Of course such titles as
these are not recognized in the aristocratic quarter
of the Faubourg St. German, nor in the provinces.
But in the Faubourg St. Honore, in the Champs
Elysee district, and around the Place de la Bourse,
soi-disant Barons, Counts, Marquesses, and even
Dukes, are as thick as flies on a hot summer day.
Of course none of these pseudo-nobles have any
documents from the French government to authen-
ticate their titles, and frequently seek to explain
their absence by the paltry and hackneyed excuse
that their " family papers were destroyed in the
revolution of 1793." This, however, can hardly

be accepted as valid, since the French monarchical governments which succeeded the Reign of Terror at the close of the last century, were exceedingly liberal—too much so, in fact—in recognizing titles which had been in existence previous to 1793. Indeed there is no excuse for a French nobleman being without some kind of a document from his government, in which his title is officially recognized.

Of the hundreds of more or less authentic Dukes to be met on the Parisian boulevards, only twenty-six have inherited their titles from a period anterior to the great revolution. They are as follows: the Dukes of Uzes, Luynes, Brissac, Richelieu, La Tremoille, Rohan, Gramont, Mortemart, Noailles, Harcourt, Fitzjames, Chaulnes, Valentinois, Praslin, La Rochefoucauld, Lorge, Broglic, Hubigny, Estissac, La Force, Maille, Clermont, Tonnevre, Sabran, Gadagne and Caderouse. Besides these there are about twenty more who owe their titles to the two Emperors Napoleon and to the two Bourbon Kings of the Restoration Louis XVIII. and Charles X. Among these are included the Dukes of Decazes, de Broglie, Rivoli, Montebello, Morny, Massena and Magenta (MacMahon). It will be seen, therefore, that the number of duly authenticated Dukes is relatively limited. Another cause, of the frequency of titles in France is

due to the fact that the old custom which pre-
vailed in the seventeenth century and according
to which the various sons of a nobleman assume
minor titles to his own in a gradation according
to their respective seniority, has been adopted with
regard to titles of the present day. Previous to
the revolution it was customary that the eldest
son of a Duke should assume during his father's
life-time the title of Prince, his next brother that
of Marquis, the third that of Count, the fourth
that of Viscount, the fifth that of Baron, the sixth
that of Chevalier, while the remaining sons had no
titles at all. This custom which was recognized
by the pre-revolution monarchy, has no *raison
d'etre* or legal basis to-day. And since it has
been adopted, not only by nobles created during
the present century, but even by the pseudo-aris-
tocracy, it will readily be understood that the
number of titled personages in France is enormous. It is hardly necessary to add that titles
confer no political or official privileges of any
kind in France of the present day.

GREAT BRITAIN.

English titles enjoy greater consideration, both
at home and abroad, than those conferred by any
other State. This is due to the fact that, although the British Empire numbers almost

300,000,000 souls, there are not more than three thousand persons bearing titles. Of these three thousands titles, which include Dukes, Marquesses, Earls, Viscounts, Barons, Baronets, Knights and the Lords Spiritual or Bishops, not more than eighteen hundred, at the very utmost, are of an hereditary nature. The remainder are titles which become extinct at the death of their present bearers. The English, Scotch, and Irish Dukes are thirty in number. Of Marquesses there are but thirty-five, of Earls three hundred and twenty-seven, of Viscounts seventy-one, and of Barons, almost four hundred. Only five hundred and forty-three of the above mentioned peers have seats in the House of Lords. The eldest sons of the Dukes, Marquesses and Earls are entitled by social courtesy and custom, but neither by legal nor official right to bear one of their father's minor titles during the life of the latter. The younger sons of Dukes and Marquesses by an act of similar social courtesy are allowed to prefix the title of Lord to their Christian name. The younger sons of Earls, and all the children of Viscounts and Barons, have no titles, but are permitted to prefix the word " Honorable " before their names. I should add that the daughters of Dukes, Marquesses, and Earls bear the courtesy of " Lady " prefixed to their Christian names. It is hardly necessary to state, that none of these courtesy titles descend to the children of their bearers, the latter having no title at all, and thus prevent the peerage from becoming overcrowded. Thus the younger son of a Duke is a plain Esquire or Mr. The same rule prevails with the royal family, and the great grandsons of the English Sovereign lose their right to be addressed as Royal Highness, and their younger sons become mere commoners. Baronets bear the title of Sir prefixed to their Christian names. The eldest sons of Baronets, the creation of whose titles is anterior to the year 1804, have the privilege of demanding Knighthood at the hands of the Sovereign on attaining their majority. This right, however, has only been once exercised during the past fifty years. Baronets have no political privileges, their rights being limited to mere precedence. Their titles are hereditary. Knights, whether they owe their title of " Sir," prefixed to their Christian name, to their membership of one of the royal orders, or to mere creation as a Knight-bachellor, bear their dignity for their life only. Their title does not descend to their son ; their wives are entitled to the prefix of " Lady " to the family name just as in the case of Baronets' wives. Marquesses, Earls, Viscounts, Barons and Bishops are invariably addressed as " My Lord " on official or ceremonious occasions, and in the same way Marchionesses, Countesses, Viscountesses, Baronesses and the wives of Baronets and Knights are addressed as " My Lady."

In conclusion it is necessary to add that with the exception of the superior grades of the British Royal Orders of Knighthood, which as stated above, entitle the holder thereof to the prefix of " Sir," there is not a single order or decoration in Europe which confers a title of any kind on its recipient. Until about six years ago the superior grades of the Austrian Orders of the Iron Crown and of the Leopold entitled their holders to the hereditary rank of Baron. But that privilege has been abolished by imperial decree.

LADY ABINGER.

Miss Helen Magruder, daughter of the late Commodore George Allen Magruder, U. S. N.

Born 1845.

Married 1863 to Lieutenant - General Lord Abinger, C. B., third Baron, a distinguished Crimean officer, born 1826.

Children:

The Honorable James Y. M. Scarlett, born March, 1871.

The Honorable Ella Scarlett, born 1864.

The Honorable Ellen Scarlett, born 1866 (married to Nicholas John Charlton, of Childwell Hall, Nottingham, and has issue):

The Honorable Evelin, born 1867 (married to Major Haverfield).

Creation of title, 1835. The first Lord Abinger was Lord Chief Baron of the Exchequer.

Seats: Inverlochy Castle, Kingussie, Inverness-shire.

Residence: 46 Cromwell Gardens, London, S. W.

MRS. JOHN T. ADAIR.

Miss Cornelia Wadsworth, daughter of the late General Wadsworth, of Genesee County, N. Y., of the United States Army, ex-War Governor of Washington, and widow of Colonel Ritchie, of Her Majesty's Army, and of Mr. John George Adair.

Born 184–.

Married 1867 to

John T. Adair, Deputy Lieutenant of Donegal, and Sheriff of the County.

Country Seats: Rathdaire and Glenveagh Castle, County Donegal, Ireland.

MARCHIONESS D'ADDA-SALVATERRA.

Miss Mary Hooper, daughter of William Hooper, Esq., of Cincinnati.

Married at Paris, 1877, to the

Marquis d'Adda-Salvaterra, of Florence.

Residence: Florence.

COMTESSE D'AVIAMON.

Miss Mary Fisher, daughter of Jones Fisher, Esq., of New York.

Married at Paris to the

Comte d'Aviamon.

Residence: Paris.

MRS. ADAM.

Miss Juliette Palmer, daughter of the late Surgeon-General Palmer, of the United States Navy.

Born 1868.

Married 1888 to

Charles Frederick Adam, Secretary to the British Embassy at Rome; born 1854; nephew of the late Right Honorable William Patrick Adam, M. P., Lord of the Treasury and Governor of Madras; and cousin of Sir Charles Adam, first Baronet.

Residence: British Embassy, Rome.

The family was founded by Archibald Adam, of Fanno, County Forfar, Scotland, in the time of King Charles I.

COUNTESS AMADEI.

Miss Mary Lewis, daughter of T. Lewis, Esq., of Connecticut.

Born 186–.

Married 188– to the

Count Amadei, formerly an officer of the Italian Army.

Residence: Rome.

DUCHESS OF ALDRAGANA AND PRINCESS CAMPOREALE.

MISS MARY BINNEY, daughter of John Binney, Esq., of Burlington, N. J.

Born 1866.

Married, first, to Thomas Kingsland, Esq., of New York, from whom she was divorced; second, in September, 1888, at Burlington, N. J. to

DON PIETRO, Prince of Camporeale, Duke of Aldragana, in the Kingdom of Sicily, born 1847, formerly in the Italian diplomatic service, son of of the late Prince Camporeale and Duke of Aldragana and of his wife Donna Laura, nee Miss Acton, who married in second marriage the late Prime Minister of Italy, Signor Minghetti.

Residence: Rome and Bologna.

MRS. ALFRED WILLIAM ANSON.

MISS GEORGIANA FRANCES GREENE, daughter of the Rev. W. Greene, of Oaklands, Virginia.

Married in 1876 to

ALFRED WILLIAM ANSON, Esq., son of the Rev. Canon Anson, of Windsor, and grandson of the late Lord Vernon.

Residence: Oaklands, Virginia.

MARCHIONESS OF ANGLESEY.

Miss Mary Living-stone King, daughter of J. P. King, Esq., of Sand-hills, Georgia, U. S. A., and widow of the Honor-able Henry Wodehouse, of England.

Married at Paris, in 1880, to

Henry Paget, fourth Marquis of Anglesey and a Baronet, Vice-Admiral for North Wales, Colonel of the Staffordshire Militia, Deputy Lieutenant for Staffordshire, who has been twice married pre-viously, and has issue by his second marriage but none by his present wife.

Seat: Baudesert, Rugely; Plass Newydd, Llan-fair, Anglesey.

Residence: 6 Avenue Montespan, Paris.

Creation of the Marquisate, 1815. The first Marquis was Viceroy of Ireland, and a celebrated Waterloo General.

VISCOMTESSE D'ANGLEMONT.

Miss Helen Thomas, daughter of the late General Thomas, U. S. A., and a niece of Pierre Lorillard, Esq., of New York.

Married at Paris to the

Viscomte Christian D'Anglemont.

Residence: Rue Lincoln, Paris.

LADY AYLMER.

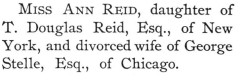

MISS ANN REID, daughter of T. Douglas Reid, Esq., of New York, and divorced wife of George Stelle, Esq., of Chicago.

Married in 1885 (as his second wife), to

SIR ARTHUR PERCY FITZ-GERALD AYLMER, of Donadea Castle, Kildare, thirteenth Baronet, born 1858, from whom she was divorced in 1886.

Residence: New York.

Creation of Baronetcy, 1621. The Aylmers settled in Ireland in the twelfth century.

MARQUISE DE SUAREZ D'AULAN.

MISS NORMA CHRISTMAS, daughter of the late J. Christmas, of Natchez, Mississippi.

Born 1858.

Married 1886, to the

MARQUIS DE SUAREZ D'AULAN, of France, formerly an officer of French cavalry.

Residence: 22 Avenue du Bois de Boulogne, Paris.

Country seat: Chateau of Aulan, Department Drome.

COUNTESS D'ARAMON.

MISS BLANCHE FISHER, daughter of the late J. Fisher, Esq., of New York.

Born 185–.

Married 187–, to

COUNT JAMES D'ARAMON, formerly an officer in the French Army.

Residence : 111 Rue de l' Universite, Paris.

———

COUNTESS DE AVENEL.

MISS MARY MEINELL, daughter of the late J. Meinell, Esq., of New York.

Born 186–.

Married 188–, to the

COUNT DE AVENEL, formerly an officer of the French Army.

Residence : 23 Rue de Galilee, Paris.

Country seat : Chateau du Champ du Genet, Department Manche, France.

———

BARONESS BAHKMETOFF.

MISS MARY BEALE, daughter of General Beale, U. S. A., of Washington.

Married to

BARON BAHKMETOFF, of Russia, formerly a Lieutenant in the Regiment of Chevaliers Gardes.

Residence: St. Petersburg.

MRS. THOMAS CHARLES BARING.

Miss Susan Carter Minturn, daughter of Robert Browne Minturn, of New York.

Married in 1859, to Thomas Charles Baring, M. P., Deputy Lieutenant for London, M. P. for London and a banker, son of the late Right Rev. Dr. Charles Baring, Lord Bishop of Durham, born 1831.

Children: Harold, born 1869.

Godfrey, 1873.

Constance.

Susannah.

Muriel.

Seat: Highbeach, Loughton, Essex.

Residence: No. 1 Grafton street, London, S. W.

The family of Baring, which is of German origin, possess the Earldom of Northbrook, created 1876; the Viscounty of Baring, created 1876; the Barony of Northbrook, created 1860; the Baronetcy of Baring, created 1793; the Barony of Ashburton, created 1835; the Barony of Revelstoke, created 1885.

BARONESS DE BAIGNE.

MISS AMELIE URQUHARDT, daughter of the late Mr. T. Urquhardt, of New Orleans, and half-sister of ex-Minister McLean.

Born 184–.

Married 186–, to

BARON de BAIGNE, formerly officer in the French Army.

Residence: Paris.

COUNTESS JOHANN HENRICH VON BERNSTORFF.

MISS ELLA LUCKERS, daughter of John Luckers, Esq., of New York.

Married at Berlin in 1888, to

COUNT JOHANN HEINRICH VON BERNSTORFF, (Stintenburg); Lieutenant in the 1st Prussian Guard Artillery Regiment, youngest son of the late Count Bernstorff, Prussian Minister of State and German Ambassador to the Court of St. James.

Creation, 1767; German and Danish Count.

COUNTESS DI BARRALHA.

MISS KATHERINE ORNE, daughter of Thomas Orne, Esq., of Germantown, Philadelphia.

Born 1857.

Married, 1877, to

COUNT DE BARRALHA, of the Kingdom of Portugal, formerly an officer in the Portuguese Army.

Residence: Palazzo Barralha, nr Agalda, Portugal.

———

MRS. BERESFORD HOPE.

MISS EVELYN FROST, daughter of General Frost, U. S. A., of St. Louis, Mo.

Born 1864.

Married, 1883, to

PHILIP BERESFORD HOPE, Justice of the Peace and Deputy Lieutenant of the County of Kent, Lord of the Manor of Beresford Hall, Staffordshire; born 1851; the son of the late Right Honorable A. J. Beresford Hope, M. P., and of the Lady Beresford Hope, sister of the Marquis of Salisbury, K. G., Prime Minister of Great Britain.

Country seat: Bedgebury Park, Cranbrook.

Town residence: 37 Montagh square, London, W.

MRS. WILLIAM GEORGE CAVENDISH-BENTINCK.

MISS ELIZABETH LIVINGSTON, daughter of Maturin Livingston, Esq., of Staatsburg, New York.

Married, in 1880, to

WILLIAM GEORGE CAVENDISH-BENTINCK, M. P. for Falmouth, great-grandson of the Duke of Portland, formerly Captain of the Dorsetshire Regiment, Justice of the Peace for Dorset, barrister-at-law, son of the Right Honorable George Augustus Frederick Cavendish-Bentinck, M. P., Privy Councillor, etc.

Issue : Mary Augusta, born 1881.

Ruth Evelyn, born 1883.

Residence: 5 Richmond Terrace, Whitehall, London, S. W. The family belongs to that of the Duke of Portland. Creation of the Duchy of Portland, 1716. The family is of Dutch origin.

BARONESS DE BREMONT.

MISS HELEN PENNIMAN, daughter of John Penniman, Esq., of New York.

Married, in 1874, to

BARON DE BREMONT, of France.

Residence: Paris.

BARONESS BERNHARD VON BEUST.

MISS SIDONIE PETERS, daughter of F. Peters, Esq., of New Albany.

Married, in 1853, to

BARON BERNHARD VON BEUST, Doctor of Medicine, born 1831.

Issue: Baron Max, 1854.

        Baron Theodore, 1871.

        Baroness Helena.

Residence: Dresden.

Ancient Saxon and Austrian Barony. A member of the family, Count Beust, was Chancellor of the Austrian Empire in 1870.

COUNTESS DE SULLY-BETHUNE.

MISS EULALIE MONTGOMERY, daughter of William Montgomery, Esq., of Louisiana.

Married, 1845, to

COUNT DE SULLY-BETHUNE, of the French Army.

Residence: 71 Rue de Lille, Paris.

Country seat. Chateau Bethancourt. Department Oise

BARONESS VON BILDT.

MISS MARY MOORE, daughter of the late J. Bloomfield Moore, Esq., of Philadelphia.

Born 1853.

Married, 1874, to

BARON CARL VON BILDT, of Sweden, formerly Secretary of the Swedish Legation at Washington, now Under-Secretary of State and Principal Secretary to H. M. King Oscar; son of General von Bildt. Prime Minister of Sweden; born 1851.

Issue: A son, born 1875.

A daughter, born 1877.

A daughter born 1878.

Residence: Stockholm.

General von Bildt, the present Premier of Sweden, was promoted by the late King from a simple private in the Guards to the rank of General and Lord High Chamberlain, and was created a Baron.

COUNTESS OF BODISCO.

MISS HARRIET WILLIAMS, daughter of J. Williams, Esq., of Georgetown, D. C.

Born 182–.

Married, 184–, to the late

COUNT DE BODISCO, Russian Minister Plenipotentiary at Washington.

Residence: St. Petersburg.

BARONESS DE BLANC.

MISS TERRY, daughter of the late Antonio Terry, of New York and Cuba.

Married, at New York, 1879, to

His Excellency BARON DE BLANC, Ambassador of the King of Italy at Constantinople, and formerly Secretary of Count Cavour, and Italian Minister to the United States.

Residence: Italian Embassy, Constantinople.

MRS. W. LANE BOOKER.

MRS. T. BISPHAM, widow of the late T. Bispham, of San Francisco, and formerly Miss Elizabeth T. Page, daughter of the late Gilbert Page, Esq., of Moorestown, N. J.

Married, 1881, to

WILLIAM LANE BOOKER, Esq., C. M. G., Her Britannic Majesty's Consul-General for the States of New York, New Jersey, Connecticut, &c.; decorated with the Order of St. Michael and St. George in 1886; born 1824. Mr. Booker held the post of H. B. M. Consul for the Pacific Coast uninterruptedly from 1857 to 1883, when he was promoted to the Consulate-General at New York.

DUCHESS AND PRINCESS OF BRANCACCIO.

MISS ELIZABETH HICKSON FIELD, daughter of J. Hickson Field, Esq., of New York and Rome.

Married, March 3, 1870, at Rome, to

DON SALVATOR BRANCACCIO, Duke of Lustra and Prince of Brancaccio, Prince of Triggiano, Marquis of Brancaccio, a Spanish Grandee of the first class; born in 1836.

The Duchess is a Lady-in-Waiting to the Queen of Italy.

Children: Don Charles, born 1870.
Donna Maria, born 1875.
Don Marc Antonio, born 1879.

Residence: Rome, Brancaccio Palace.

Creation of Prince, 1391; of Duke, 1625.

COMTESSE DE LA BOISSIERE.

MISS MARGARET DUNLAP, daughter of James Dunlap, Esq., of Louisville, Kentucky.

Married, at Long Branch, to the

COMTE DE LA BOISSIERE, of Paris, Syndic of the Foreign Press at Paris.

Residence: 89 Rue de Grenelle, Paris.

LADY BURNETT.

MISS MATILDA JOSEPH-INE MURPHY, daughter of the late James Murphy, Esq., of New York.

Married, in 1864, to

SIR ROBERT BURNETT, of Leys, Kincaidineshire, eleventh Baronet, born in 1833. Deputy Lieutenant for Kincaidineshire. No issue.

Seat: Crathes Castle, near Aberdeen.

Residence: 3 Charles st., Berkeley square.

Creation, 1626. The estates are held under a charter signed by King Robert Bruce, 1324. The first Baronet was an intimate friend of King Charles I.

COUNTESS DE BRAZZA-SAVORGNAN.

MISS CORA SLOCOMB, daughter of Cuthbert Slocomb, Esq., of New York.

Married, at New York, October 18, 1887, to

COUNT DETALMA DE BRAZZA-SAVORGNAN, of Italy.

Residence: Rome.

The Count is a cousin of the well-known African explorer.

BARONESS ALBERT VON BULOW.

Miss Adele A. Ward, daughter of General R. C. Ward, of New York.

Born in 1863.

Married, in 1885, to

Baron Albert von Bulow, Lieutenant in the Second Regiment of Fusilier Guards at Berlin, and son of the late Secretary of State and Cabinet Minister von Bulow.

———

COUNTESS OF BUXHOFWDEN.

Miss Caroline McKnight, daughter of John McKnight, Esq., of Bordentown, New Jersey.

Born 1827.

Married, in 1847, to

The late Count Constantine Buxhoewden of Russia ; born February, 1824.

The Countess is aunt of the present head of the family.

Creation: Russian Count, 1797 ; Prussian Count, 1795 ; belongs to the Livonian nobility. Ancient Saxon family.

LADY ARTHUR BUTLER.

MISS ELLEN STAGER, daughter of the late General Anson Stager, U. S. A., of Chicago.

Married, in 1877, to

LORD JAMES ARTHUR WELLINGTON FOLEY BUTLER, second son of the second Marquis of Ormonde and heir presumptive to his brother the present Marquis, who is without male issue; born September, 1849; formerly Lieutenant First Life Guards, formerly State Steward to the Viceroy of Ireland, is an M. A. of Trinity College, Cambridge.

Residence: London.

Creation of Marquisate, 1825.

The family hold the Hereditary Chief Butlership of Ireland, and is descended from Theobald Fitzwalter, who accompanied King Henry II to Ireland in 1177, when he was created Hereditary Chief Butler.

————

PRINCESS CAMPOREALE.

(See Duchess of Aldragana.)

BARONESS DE BRIN.

Miss Anita Ledoux, daughter of Mr. Ledoux, of New Orleans.

Born 1854.

Married, at Paris, 1886, to

Baron Leon de Brin, Minister Plenipotentiary in the French Diplomatic Service.

Residence: 12 Avenue Kleber, Paris.

Country seat: Chateau de Beau Solleil, Loire Inferieure.

MARCHIONESS DE CALDERON DE BARCA.

Miss Helen McLaw, daughter of John McLaw, Esq., of Staten Island.

Married, in 1879, to the

Marquis de Calderon de Barca of Spain.

Residence: Madrid.

DUCHESS OF CAMPOSELICE.

Widow of the late Isaac Singer.

Married, 1886, to the late

Duke of Camposelice of Amsterdam, who was created Duke by the Papal Government in 1876, and died September 1887.

Seat: Chateau de Bloseville, Normandy.

Residence: Avenue Kleber, Paris.

THE HON. MRS. WILLIAM CARRINGTON.

MISS JULIET WARDEN, daughter of Francis Warden, of New York.

Born 1852.

Married, 1871, to Colonel the HONORABLE WILLIAM H. PEREGRINE CARRINGTON, second son of the second Lord Carrington, and brother and heir presumptive to the present peer. Colonel Carrington is Equerry to Her Majesty Queen Victoria, and holds the Secretaryship of the Lord Great Chamberlain's Office. He was born in 1845, and served with distinction in the Egyptian campaign, as Colonel of the Grenadier Guards.

No issue.

Country seat: Burfield, Old Windsor.

Town residence: Royal Court, House of Lords, Westminster.

The Peerage of Carrington was conferred in 1779 on Robert Smith, the famous Nottingham Banker.

COUNTESS CASA DE AGREDA.

Widow of George L. Lorillard, Esq., of New York, and divorced wife of Edward Wight, Esq., of New York.

Married, 1889, to
COUNT CASA DE AGREDA, of Spain.
Residence: Paris.

———

COMTESSE DE CASTIGLIONNE.

MISS ELLA PORTER, daughter of W. Porter, Esq., of Newport, R. I.

Married to the
COUNT DE CASTIGLIONNE.
Residence: Paris.

———

COUNTESS CERATI DI CALRY.

MISS ELLEN F. ABBOTT, daughter of Redman Abbott, Esq., of Philadelphia.

Married, August 12, 1880, to
COUNT VALERIO MAGAWLY CERATI DI CALRY, a Count of the Holy Roman Empire.
Residence: Cerati, in Italy.

COUNTESS DE ROHAN CHABOT.

MRS. HERBERT GALLATIN, widow of the late Herbert Gallatin, Esq., of New York.

Born 183–.

Married, at Paris, June, 1875, to the COUNT AUGUSTE DE ROHAN CHABOT.

Residence: 8 Rue Portalis, Paris.

MRS. JOSEPH CHAMBERLAIN.

MISS MARY ENDICOTT, daughter of W. C. Endicott, Esq., Secretary of War at Washington, from 1885 to 1889.

Born 1866.

Married, 1888, at Washington, to

The Right Honorable JOSEPH CHAMBERLAIN, M. P.; Privy Councilor, President of the Board of Trade, and of the Local Government Board in Mr. Gladstone's Liberal Cabinet from 1880 to 1886; Ambassador Extraordinary and High Commissioner to Washington for the settlement of the Fisheries disputes between the United States and Canada; born 1836; son of the late Joseph Chamberlain. Mr. Chamberlain has been twice previously married.

Country seat: Highbury, Moor Green, Birmingham.

Town residence: 40 Princes Gardens, London, S. W.

BARONESS DE CHARETTE.

Miss Mary Polk, daughter of Colonel A. J. Polk, of Nashville, Tenn., and granddaughter of Bishop Polk, who was killed in battle during the Civil War.

Born 1857.

Married, in 1879, at Paris, to

General Baron de Charette, the famous French General, who distinguished himself as Colonel of the Papal Zouaves at Rome, and subsequently in the Franco-Prussian War of 1870. The General has children by his first wife, who was a daughter of the Duke of Fitzjames. The De Charettes are an ancient family of the Vendee, and won great fame as leaders of the Royalists in the Vendean War of 1797.

Residence: Avenue Hoche, Paris.

Country seat: Chateau De La Basse-Mothe, Brittany.

COUNTESS OF CIBO.

Miss Mary Walker, daughter of the late J. Walker, Esq., of Philadelphia.

Born 185–.

Married, 187–, to the

Comte de Cibo, of Italy, formerly an officer in the Italian Army.

Residence: Rome.

MRS. CHARLES PELHAM-CLINTON.

 MISS LIZZIE ZEREGA, daughter of J. Zerega, Esq., of New York.

Born in 1867.

Married, in 1886, at New York, to

CHARLES STAPLETON PELHAM-CLINTON, formerly Lieutenant of the Leinster Regiment, son of Lord Charles Pelham-Clinton, and grandson of the fourth Duke of Newcastle ; born 1857.

Residence : New York.

The Duchy of Newcastle was created in 1756.

COUNTESS DE CHABOT.

MISS MARY HEYWARD, daughter of the late J. Heyward, Esq., of New York.

Born 185–.

Married, 187–, to the

COUNT DE CHABOT, formerly an officer in the French Army.

Residence: 17 Boulevard de Madelaine, Paris.

Country seat: Chateau de Vinde, Department Marine, France.

MRS. WILLIAM OSWALD CHARLTON.

Miss Mary Grant, daughter of Archibald Grant, Esq., of Washington, D. C.

Born 1854.

Married, 1873, to

William Oswald Charlton, Esq., Justice of the Peace and Deputy Lieutenant of the County of Northumberland; born 1850; son W. H. Charlton, Esq., who died in 1880.

Country seat: Hesleyside, Bellingham, England.

MARQUISE DE CHASSELOUP-LAUBAT.

Miss Pilie, daughter of the late J. Pilie, Esq., of New Orleans.

Born 185–.

Married, in 187–, to the late

Marquis de Chasseloup-Laubat, formerly an officer in the French Navy.

Town residence: 51 Avenue Kleber, Paris.

Country seat: Chateau de la Gataudiere, Department Charente, France.

LADY RANDOLPH CHURCHILL, C. I.

MISS JENNIE JEROME, daughter of Leonard Jerome, Esq., of New York.

Born 1853.

Married, 1874, to the

Right Honorable LORD RANDOLPH HENRY CHURCHILL; born 1849; the second son of the late Duke of Marlborough, and brother of the present Duke. Lord Randolph is M. P. for Paddington, a Privy Councilor, and has held the office of Chancellor of the Exchequer and of Secretary of State for India, is a D. C. L. of Cambridge University, a Deputy Lieutenant for Oxfordshire, &c.

Children: Winston Leonard, born 1874.

John Henry, born 1880.

Residence: No. 2 Connaught place, London.

(For creation of title and descent of family, see Marlborough.)

Lady Randolph Churchill has had conferred upon her by the Queen, the Imperial Order of the Crown of India.

VICOMTESSE DE COETLEGEN.

MISS MARY BLAKE, daughter of the late J. Blake, Esq., of Boston.

Married, in 1864, at Paris, to the late

VICOMTE DE COETLEGEN, an officer in the French Army.

Residence: Paris.

PRINCESS GALATRO COLONNA.

Miss Eva Julia Bryant (Mackay), step-daughter of John W. Mackay, Esq., President of the Nevada Bank, San Francisco, and of the Commercial Cable Co., &c.

Born November 12, 1861, at San Francisco.

Married, February 11, 1885, at Paris, to

Don Ferdinand Colonna, Prince of Galatro, Prince of Paliano, Prince of Colonna and Prince of Stigliano, a Spanish Grandee of the First Class, and an officer of the Italian Cavalry; born 1858; eldest son of Don Joachim Colonna, who is heir to Don Marc Antonio Colonna, fifth Prince of Stigliano and chief of the Stigliano branch of the Colonna family.

Issue: one son, born 1886.

Creations of titles: Prince of Galatro of the Kingdom of Naples, 1688; Prince of Stigliano, 1716; Prince of Paliano, 1716; Prince of the Empire, 1710.

Residence: 52 Avenue du Bois de Bologne, Paris.

LADY COOK.

(Viscountess of Montserrat in the Peerage of Portugal.)

MISS JENNIE CLAFFIN, daughter of R. B. Claffin, Esq., of New York.

Married, in London, 1885, as his second wife, to

SIR FRANCIS COOK, Baronet and Viscount of Montserrat in the Peerage of Portugal; born 1817; created Baronet in 1886; is a member of the firm of Messrs. Cook, Son & Co., of St. Paul's Churchyard.

Residences: Doughty House, Richmond, Surrey; Montserrat, Cintra, Portugal.

Sir Francis has two sons and a daughter by his first marriage.

MADAME CLEMENCEAU.

MISS MARY PLUMMER, daughter of J. Plummer, Esq., of New York.

Married, at New York by Mayor Oakey Hall, in 1869, to

M. GEORGE CLEMENCEAU, the celebrated French statesman, a Member of the Chamber of Deputies, leader of the Radical party in France, and Editor of *La Justice*.

Residence: Rue Clement-Marot, Paris.

THE HON. MRS. CHARLES SPENCER-COWPER.

MISS JESSIE McLEAN, daughter of the late Colonel Clinton McLean, U. S. A., of Newburgh, N. Y.

Born 1850.

Married, 1871, to

The late Hon. CHARLES SPENCER-COWPER, younger son of the fifth Earl of Cowper, who was a Prince of the Holy Roman Empire. The Hon. Charles Cowper died in 1879.

Residence: London.

The family was founded in 1642 by Sir William Cowper, the favorite companion of King Charles I. The Earldom was created in 1718.

MRS. COSTELLOE.

MISS MARY WHITEALL SMITH, daughter of R. Pearsall Smith, Esq., of Philadelphia.

Born 1863.

Married, in 1875, to

BENJAMIN F. C. COSTELLOE, Barrister-at-Law. He unsuccessfully contested for the seat in Parliament for Edinburgh, on the Liberal ticket, at the general election of 1886; born 1854; son of the late M. R. Costelloe, Esq., of H. M. Board of Trade.

MRS. EDWARD DENMAN THORNBURGH-CROPPER.

MISS VIRGINIA S. THORNBURGH, daughter of William B. Thornburgh, of Virginia and San Francisco.

Born 1855.

Married, 1874, to Captain EDWARD DENMAN THORNBURGH-CROPPER, Captain in Royal Artillery; born in 1854.

The first Lord Denman was Lord Chief Justice of England, and the defender of Queen Caroline in the divorce suit brought against her by her husband, King George IV. of Great Britain.

VISCOUNTESS DE COURVAL.

MISS RAY, daughter of Mr. Ray, of Philadelphia.

Born 185–.

Married, at Paris, 187–, to the

VISCOUNT DE COURVAL, formerly an officer in the French Army.

Residence: 6 Rue Fortin, Paris.

Country seat: Chateau de Pinon, Anizy, Aisne, France.

THE DUCHESS DECAZES AND OF GLUCKS-BJERG.

Miss Isabella Singer, daughter of the late Isaac Singer, Esq., of sewing-machine fame.

Born 1869.

Married, at Paris, April 28, 1888, at the Church of St. Pierre de Chaillot, to

Jean Elie, Duke of Decazes and Glucksbjerg, in the Peerages of France and Denmark; born 1864; son of the late Duke Louis, the well-known Minister of Foreign Affairs of the Third Republic, who died September 16, 1886.

Residence: 36 Avenue de Jena, Paris.

Country seat: Chateau de la Grave, Gironde, France.

Creation, 1815. The first Duke was the confidant and Minister of Police of King Louis XVIII.

COUNTESS DE DOMPIERRE.

Miss Mary Corbin, daughter of Francis P. Corbin, Esq., of Virginia.

Born 185–.

Married, 187–, to the

Comte de Dompierre, formerly an officer of the French Navy.

Residence: Paris.

MRS. ERNEST W. BECKETT-DENNISON.

 MISS LUCY TRACY LEE, daughter of the late William P. Lee, Esq., of New York.

Married, in 1883, to

Captain ERNEST WILLIAM BECKETT-DENNISON, Esq., M. P.; born in 1856; is a member of the banking firm of Beckett & Co.; eldest son of William Beckett, M. P., who is heir to the Barony and Baronetcy of Grimthorpe, now held by his elder brother, the first Lord Grimthorpe.

Seat: Kirkstall Grange, near Leeds.

Residence: 138 Piccadilly.

Creation of Baronetcy, 1813; of Barony, 1886.

MRS. ARCHIBALD C. D. DICK.

MISS ISABELLE PARROTT, daughter of the late J. Parrott, Esq., of San Francisco.

Married, 1883, to

ARCHIBALD C. D. DICK, Esq., grandson of the late Sir Francis Walker-Drummond, Bart.

Residence: 58 Onslow Gardens, London.

Creation of Baronetcy, 1827.

COUNTESS DE DIESBACH DE BELLE-
ROCHE.

Miss Meta McCall, daughter of the late —
McCall, Esq., of Philadelphia.

Born 1853.

Married, September 19, 1871, at Geneva, to

Count Alfons de Deisbach de Belleroche;
born March, 1847; formerly in the French Diplomatic Service.

Issue: Ladislaus, born January, 1874.

Residence: 12 Avenue Bugeaud, Paris; and
Nice.

Creation as French Count, 1747.

DUCHESS DE DINO.

Miss Adele Sampson, daughter of the late
Joseph Sampson, Esq., of New York. Divorced
wife of Frederick Livingston, Esq.

Married, as second wife, January 25, 1887, to

Maurice, Marquis of Talleyrand-Perigord, Duke
of Dino, to whom his father, authorized by the
President of the French Republic, ceded on January 25, 1887, his title of Duke of Dino; he is the
son of the Marquis Alexander, of Tallyrand-Perigord, Duke of Dino, who is the brother of the Duke
of Tallyrand, Duke of Sagan, Duke of Valencay,
Knight of the Golden Fleece, and the head of the
family.

Residence: Paris.

The Duke has issue by his first marriage.

COUNTESS OF EDLA.

MISS ELISE HENSLER, daughter of — Hensler, Esq., of Boston.

Born 1836.

Married, morganatically, June 10, 1869, to the late

King-Consort, FERDINAND OF PORTUGAL; widow, December 17, 1885.

Residence: Lisbon.

County seat: Chateau of Cintra, Portugal.

Miss Elise Hensler was one of the earliest of the American prima-donnas. She made her debut in New York twenty-five years ago. She was afterward engaged for the Royal Opera-House, at Lisbon, where Prince Ferdinand of Saxe-Coburg-Gotha, the husband of Donna Maria de Gloria, Queen Regnant of Portugal and father of the present King, espoused her morganatically after the death of the Queen. He conferred upon her the title of Countess of Edla, in the Duchy of Saxe-Coburg-Gotha (June 10, 1862). She has always been treated with great consideration by the Royal family. Since the death of her husband, a few years ago, the Countess has lived in strict retirement at Cintra.

BARONESS ERLANGER.

MISS SLIDELL, daughter of the late — Slidell, Esq., of Virginia.

Married to

BARON ERLANGER, of the well-known banking house of that name, and Consul-General of Greece, at Paris.

Address: 20 Rue Taitbout, Paris.

Country Residence: Villa Erlanger, Deauville, France.

———

COUNTESS MAXIMILIAN ESTERHAZY-GALANTHA.

MRS. CHARLES GRIFFIN, widow of the late Major-General Charles Griffin, U. S. A., and formerly Miss Sarah Virginia Carroll, daughter of the late — Carroll, Esq.,

Born 1840.

Married, in 1869, to the late

COUNT MAXIMILIAN ERNST MARIA ESTER-HAZY-GALANTHA (of the Forchtienstein branch), born 1837; died 1883.

This branch of the Princely House of Esterhazy possesses the title of Count since 1626.

Residence: Washington.

LADY FAIRFAX.

Miss Mary Kirby, daughter of Colonel Edmund Kirby, U. S. A.

Married, in 1857, to

Dr. John Contee Fairfax, Lord Fairfax, eleventh Baron; born 1830.

Issue:

The Hon. Albert Kirby Fairfax, born June 23, 1870.

The Hon. Charles Edmund Kirby Fairfax, born 1876.

The Hon. Caroline Fairfax, born 1858.

The Hon. Josephine Fairfax, born 1865.

The Hon. Mary Fairfax, born 1871.

The Hon. Frances Fairfax, born 1878.

Residence: Northampton, Bladensburg, Prince George County, Maryland.

Creation of Barony, 1627. The third Baron was the celebrated General of Cromwell's forces which defeated King Charles I. at Marston Moor.

LADY FAIRFAX (Dowager).

Miss Ada Benham, daughter of the late Joseph S. Benham, Esq., of Cincinnati, Ohio.

Married, in 1845, to the late

Lord Fairfax, who died in 1869.

No issue.

Residence: Ranche San Marin, California.

(For family, see Lady Fairfax.)

VISCOUNTESS FALKLAND.

MISS MARY READE, daughter of the late Robert Reade, Esq., of New York.

Born 1858.

Married, in 1879, to Colonel LORD FALK-LAND, twelfth Viscount; born 1845; succeeded 1886; served in the English Army.

Issue:

The Hon. Lucius Cary, Master of Falkland, born 1880.

The Hon. Byron, born 1887.

The Hon. Catherine, born 1882.

The Hon. Mary, born 1884.

Country seat: South Norwood Hill, Surrey, England.

The family was founded and the Peerage granted in 1620.

COUNTESS DE DION.

MISS AMELIE McCARTHY, daughter of J. W. McCarthy, Esq., of New York.

Born 186–.

Married, 188–, to the late

COMTE DE DION.

Residence: 68 Rue Babylon, Paris.

VICOMTESSE DE FONTENILLIAT.

Miss Mimi Smith, daughter of S. Smith, Esq., of Mobile, Ala., and sister of Mrs. W. K. Vanderbilt, of New York.

Born 1857.

Married, at Paris, December, 1887, to

Vicomte Gaston de Fontenilliat, of Paris, formerly in the French Army.

Residence : New York.

MRS. FRANCKLYN.

Miss Susan G. Hoyt, daughter of Edwin Hoyt, Esq., of New York.

Married, in 1869, to

Charles Gilbert Francklyn, Esq., of London and New York; a cousin of Sir Bache Cunard.

COUNTESS DE FRUSAC.

Miss Thorne, daughter of — Thorne, Esq., West Sixteenth st., New York.

Married to the

Count de Frusac, of France.

Residence : Paris.

MRS. MORETON FREWEN.

MISS JEROME, daughter of Leonard Jerome, Esq., of New York.

Married, in 1879, to

MORETON FREWEN, Justice of the Peace and Deputy Lieutenant of the County of Sussex; third son of Thomas Frewen, Esq., M. P., of Brickwall, Sussex; born 1853.

Residence: 18 Alford st., Mayfair, London.

Country seat: Clifden Lodge, Galway.

The Frewens are one of the most ancient and influential families of Sussex.

MME. VON FRIEDLAENDER.

MISS WHEELRIGHT, daughter of — Wheelright, Esq., of New York.

Married to

HERR VON FRIEDLAENDER, of Berlin.

COUNTESS DE GANEY.

MISS RIDGEWAY, daughter of — Ridgeway, Esq., of Philadelphia.

Married to the

COMTE DE GANEY, of Paris.

COUNTESS GIANOTTI.

Miss Constance Kinney, daughter of J. Kinney, Esq., of New Jersey.

Born 1854.

Married, in 1872, to

Count Cæsar Gianotti, the Grand Master of Ceremonies at the Court of the Quirinal, Rome.

Issue: two daughters, who are both god-children of Queen Margherita of Italy.

COUNTESS DE GHERANDESCHI.

Miss Fisher, daughter of Jones Fisher, Esq., of New York.

Born 185–.

Married, in 187–, to the

Count Gherandeschi, of Rome.

Residence: Rome.

Count Gherandeschi is a lineal descendant of the Count Ugolini, whose tragic story is related by Dante in his Inferno.

BARONESS VON GLUMER.

Senora Oviedo, widow of Senor Oviedo, of Cuba, and formerly Miss Bartlett, daughter of — Bartlett, Esq., of New York.

Married to

Baron von Glumer, of Berlin.

LADY GRAHAM OF ESK.

Miss Eliza Jane Burn, daughter of Charles Burn, Esq., of New York.

Married, in 1874, to

Sir Robert James Stuart Graham, of Esk, Cumberland; tenth Baronet.

Residence: Brooklyn, N. Y.

Creation of title, 1629. The first Baronet was Gentleman of the Horse to King James I.

COUNTESS DE GABRIAC.

Miss Florence Phalen, daughter of James Phalen, of New York, and of Paris.

Born 1842.

Married, in 1861, to the late

Count Horace de Cadoine de Gabriac, an officer in the French Army.

Issue: Mathilde de Gabriac, who is married to the Marquis de Gabriac, formerly French Ambassador at Rome.

Residence: 23 Rue de Bassins, Paris.

MRS. HUGH GRAHAM.

Miss Jessie Low, daughter of the late Andrew Low, Esq., of Savannah, Ga.

Born 1870.

Married, November 24, 1888, in London, to

Hugh Graham, Esq., second son of the late Sir Frederick Graham, of Netherby, England, and brother of the fourth Baronet of that name.

Residence : London.

The Baronetcy was created in 1783, and the second Baronet was the Secretary of State for War during the Crimean campaign.

BARONESS GOMEZ.

Miss Louise Hatcher, daughter of the late John Hatcher, Esq., of Indiana.

Born 1866.

Married, in 1886, at Washington, to

Baron Gomez, of Brazil, Envoy Extraordinary and Minister Plenipotentiary of the Empire of Brazil, at Rome.

Residence: Brazilian Legation, Rome.

LADY GRANTLEY.

MISS KATHERINE McVICKER, daughter of William Henry McVicker, Esq., of New York, and divorced wife of Major Charles Grantley-Norton, of the Twenty-third Fusiliers (who is the uncle of her present husband).

Married, November 5, 1879, to JOHN RICHARD BRINSLEY NORTON, Lord Grantley, fifth Baron; born 1855; Deputy-Lieutenant for the County of York, England.

Issue:

The Hon. Joan Norton, born November 10, 1879.

The Hon. Eleanor Norton.

The Hon. Winnifred Norton, twins, born 1881.

The Hon. Katherine Norton, born 1883.

Seats: Grantley Hall, Ripon, Yorkshire; Kettlethorp Hall, Wakefield, Yorkshire.

Residence: 26 Hertford St., Mayfair, London.

The Barony of Grantley was created in 1782. The first Baron was Speaker of the House of Commons.

BARONESS DE LA GRANGE.

MISS E. CARROLL, daughter of Thomas Carroll, Esq., of Virginia, and granddaughter of Royal Phelps, Esq.

Born 185–.

Married, in 187–, at Paris, to
BARON LOUIS DE LA GRANGE.

Residence : 63 Avenue Alma, Paris.

LADY VERNON HARCOURT.

MRS. J. P. IVES, widow of J. P. Ives, Esq., and formerly Miss Elizabeth Motley, daughter of the Hon. J. Lothrop Motley, historian, formerly United States Minister to the Hague and Vienna.

Married, (as second wife) in 1876, to the
Right Honorable SIR WILLIAM GEORGE GRANVILLE VENABLES VERNON HARCOURT, M. P., Q. C., Privy Councilor ; born 1827 ; late Solicitor-General; late Secretary of State for the Home Department; late Chancellor of the Exchequer; knighted in 1873.

Issue by his first marriage :
    Louis, born in 1863.
By his second marriage :
    Robert, born 1878.
Seat : Malwood, Lindhurst, Hants.
Residence : 7 Grafton St., London.
(Belongs to the family of Lord Vernon.)

THE HON. MRS. RALPH HARBORD.

MISS ELIZABETH SHENLEY, daughter of the late E. W. H. Shenley, Esq., of New York, and London.

Born 1844.

Married, in 1865, to the late

Hon. RALPH HARBORD, sixth son of the third Lord Suffield, who died in 1878.

Issue:

> Edward Ralph, born 1870.
> Horatio, born 1875.
> Florence Mary, born 1866.
> Agnes Georgiana, born 1871.
> Emily Fanny, born 1873.
> Ida, born 1878.

Residence : Princes Gate, London, S. W.

The head of the house of Harbord is Lord Suffield, K. C. B., fifth Baron, and a Baronet of Gunton Park, Norfolk. He is Lord in Waiting to the Prince of Wales. The Baronetcy was conferred in 1745, and the Peerage in 1786.

MRS. HUGHES-HALLET.

MISS EMILY SCHAUMBERG, daughter of the late Colonel Schaumberg, of Philadelphia, U. S.

Married, in London, 1882, as second wife, to

Lieutenant-Colonel F. C. HUGHES-HALLET, formerly Conservative Member of Parliament for Rochester; late Captain Royal Artillery, Lieutenant-Colonel of Volunteers; born 1838; entered Royal Artillery 1859; married 1871, to Lady Selwyn (widow of the late Lord Justice Selwyn), who died in 1875.

Residence: 108 Cromwell Road. London.

LADY HORNBY.

MISS EMILY AUGUSTA ROBERTS, daughter of John Pratt Roberts, Esq., New York.

Married, in 1875 (as third wife), to

SIR EDMUND HORNBY, Knight, born 1825, and was Chief Judge of the Supreme Court of China and Japan until 1876.

Residence: 10 Wellswood Park, Torquay, and Lensden House, Dartmoor.

Created Knight 1862.

THE HON. MRS. MICHAEL HERBERT.

MISS BELLE WILSON, daughter of — Wilson, Esq., of New York.

Married, in 1888, to the Hon. MICHAEL HENRY HERBERT, youngest brother of the Earl of Pembroke, and son of the late Lord Herbert, of Lea, the well-known British Statesman and Minister; born 1857; is a second Secretary of Her Britannic Majesty's Embassy at Paris.

Residence: British Legation, Washington.

The present Earl of Pembroke is the thirteenth in direct line of succession, besides being the tenth Earl of Montgomery, and the second Lord Herbert of Lea.

The Earldom of Pembroke was created in 1549; that of Montgomery in 1605. The first Earl was a celebrated General and Governor of the, at that time, British port of Calais.

BARONESS HIRSCH.

MISS MARIE PILIE, daughter of the late J. Pilie, Esq., of New Orleans.

Born 185–.

Married, 187–, to

BARON E. HIRSCH, of Paris.

Residence: Champs Elysees, Paris.

MRS. HENRY HOWARD.

MISS CECILIA RIGGS, daughter of George W. Riggs, Esq., of Washington.

Married, in 1867, to HENRY HOWARD, Esq., C. B., First Secretary of the British Legation at Pekin, formerly Secretary of the British Legation at Washington; decorated with the Order of the Bath in 1875; son of Sir Henry Howard, G. C. B., formerly Envoy to Brazil and Bavaria; born 1843;

Issue:

George, born 1869.
Henry, born 1873.
Marie, born 1868.
Janet, born 1871.
Alice, born 1876.

Residence : British Legation, Pekin.

Mr. Howard is cousin and collateral to the present (fifteenth) Duke of Norfolk, who is Premier Peer of the Realm, and Hereditary Earl Marshal and Chief Butler of England. The title of Duke was conferred in the year 1483.

COUNTESS HATZFELDT.

Miss Helen Moulton, daughter of Charles Frederick Moulton, Esq.

Born September, 3, 1846.

Married, at Paris, in 1863, to

Count Paul Von Hatzfeldt-Wildenburg, German Ambassador to the Court of St. James, and late Secretary of State for Foreign Affairs at Berlin; Knight of Malta; born 1831.

Issue:

        Countess Helen, born March, 1865.

        Count Paul, born June, 1867.

        Countess Marie, born January, 1871.

Creation as Count of the German Empire, 1635.

Residence: German Embassy, London.

The Count and Countess of Hatzfeldt were divorced in the year 1874, but were reconciled and re-married at Baden-Baden in September, 1889.

BARONESS HOYNINGEN-HUENE.

Miss Emily Lothrop, daughter of George V. N. Lothrop, formerly United States Minister at St. Petersburg.

Born 1868.

Married, 1888, at New York, to the

Baron Barthold von Hoyningen-Huene, Captain of the Regiment of Chevalier Gardes of the Empress of Russia.

Residence: St. Petersburg.

LADY FERMOR-HESKETH.

 Miss Florence Emily Sharon, daughter of the late Senator William Sharon, of Nevada.

Born 186–.

Married, in 1880, to

Sir Thomas George Fermor Fermor-Hesketh, seventh Baronet; born May 9, 1849; is Major of Fourth Battalion, King's Regiment; has been Sheriff of Northamptonshire, and is a Deputy Lieutenant and Justice of the Peace of the County.

Issue:

   Thomas, born November 17, 1881.

   Frederick, born 1883.

Seats: Rufford Hall, Ormskirk, and Easton Neston, Towcester.

Creation of title, 1761.

The family has been settled in Lancashire for seven hundred years.

COUNTESS KESSLER.

Miss Wickershaw, daughter of — Wickershaw, Esq., of New York.

Married to

Count Kessler, of Hamburg.

Residence: 30 Coursla Reine, Paris.

COUNTESS VON HEUSSENSTAMM ZU HEIS-SENSTEIN AND GRAFENHAUSEN, BAR-ONESS OF STARHEMBERG.

Miss Agnes Carroll, daughter of the late Albert Carroll, Esq., of Doughoregen Manor, Virginia.

Born January 15, 1863, at Baltimore.

Married, April 13, 1887, from the United States Legation at Vienna, by the Papal Nuncio, to

Count Anton Otto von Heussenstamm zu Heissenstein and Grafenhausen, Baron of Starhemberg; born April 13, 1856; a Chamberlain of the Austrian Emperor, and Junior Captain of the Seventh Regiment of Austrian Uhlans.

The family of Heussenstamm possesses the title of Baron since 1571, and that of Count since June 27, 1637.

_____

LADY KORTRIGHT.

Miss Martha Ellen Richardson, daughter of the late John Richardson, Esq., Governor of the Bank of North America, Philadelphia.

Born 183–.

Married, in 1862, to the late

Sir Charles Edward Keith Kortright, Her Majesty's Consul at Philadelphia; born 1813; knighted 1886; died 1888.

Residence: 2 Grosvenor Crescent, Belgrave Square, London.

LADY LISTER-KAYE.

 Miss Natica Yznaga del Valle, daughter of Senor Antonio Yznaga del Valle, of Ravenswood, La., and Cuba.

Married, in 1881, to

Sir John Pepys Lister-Kaye, of Derby Grange, Yorkshire, third Baronet; born 1853; formerly Lieutenant of the Royal Horse Guards; Deputy-Lieutenant for the County of Yorkshire.

Creation, 1812.

The family is asserted to be descended from Sir Kaye, an ancient Briton, one of the Knights of the Round Table.

COUNTESS DE KERGOLAY.

Miss Carroll, daughter of Thomas Carroll, Esq., of Virginia.

Born 185–.

Married, 18—, to the

Comte Jean de Kergolay, of Brittany, formerly an officer in the French Army.

Residence: 17 Rue Matignon, Paris.

MRS. ARTHUR CLARK-KENNEDY.

MISS ALICE APPLETON, daughter of — Appleton Esq., of Boston.

Married, at Boston, to

ARTHUR CLARK-KENNEDY, Esq., son of the late Colonel John Clark-Kennedy, of Knockgray, and grandson of Sir Alexander Clark-Kennedy.

Residence : Park Lane, London.

BARONESS KLENCK.

MISS ARNALIE MEINELL, daughter of the late J. Meinell, Esq., of New York.

Born 186–.

Married, in 188–, to the late

BARON KLENCK.

Residence : 26 Avenue Marceau, Paris.

BARONESS VON KUBECK VON KUBAN.

MISS MARY LOUSAY, daughter of — Lousay, Esq., of New Orleans.

Born 184–.

Married, in 1868, to

Privy Chancellor BARON J. KUBECK VON KUBAN, Governor of the Austrian Province of Styria.

The Baroness is a sister of Mrs. Consul-General Havemeyer, of New York.

LADY LAMPSON (Dowager).

 Miss Jane Sibley, daughter of the late Gibbs Sibley, Esq., of Sutton, Mass.

Born 1809.

Married, in 1827, to the late Sir Curtis Miranda Lampson, first Baronet, who died in 1885.

Issue:

Sir George Curtis Lampson, second Baronet, born 1833, who is married and has issue.

Country seat: Rowfant, Crawley, Sussex.

Residence: 80 Eaton Square, London.

Creation of Baronetcy, 1866.

The first Baronet was a native of New Haven, Vt., United States, who was naturalized as a British subject in 1848, and received his title for his services as Chairman of the Atlantic Telegraph Company in laying the first successful transatlantic cable.

BARONESS VON LAGERFELDT.

Miss — Day, daughter of — Day, Esq., of Steubenville, Ohio.

Born 185–.

Married, in 187–, to

Baron von Lagerfeldt, of Sweden.

Residence: Stockholm.

COUNTESS DE LA BASSETIERE.

Miss Alice O'Donnell, daughter of J. O'Donnell, Esq., of Baltimore, and a niece of Governor John Lee Carroll.

Born 1860.

Married, in 1888, to the

Comte de la Bassetiere, formerly an officer in the French Army.

Residence: Paris.

Country seat: Chateau de Saumery.

DUCHESS OF LANTE MONFELTRIO DELLA ROVERE.

Miss Mathilde Davis, daughter of Thomas Davis, Esq., of New York.

Born, New York, 1847.

Married, April 25, 1866, to

Don Antonio, Duke of Lante Monfeltrio della Rovere, Duke of San Croce di Magliano, Spanish Grandee of the first class; born at Rome April 5, 1831.

Issue:

> Don Pietro, born March 30, 1867,
> And five other children.

Residence: Villa Lante, of Bagnaja, near Viterbo.

The Duchess owns large estates on Nassau, Pine, Broad, and other down-town streets in New York.

MARQUISE DE LANZA.

MISS MARY HAMMOND, daughter of Dr. William A. Hammond, of New York and Washington.

Born 185–.

Married, in 188–, to the

MARQUIS DE LANZA, of Italy.

Residence: New York.

———

BARONESS LA TOURNELLE.

MISS ELIZABETH MEINELL, daughter of the late J. Meinell, Esq., of New York.

Born 186–.

Married, in 188–, to the

BARON LA TOURNELLE, formerly an officer in the French Army.

Residence: 2 Rue Lincoln, Paris.

Country seat: Chateau de Fargot, Department Loire et Cher, France.

———

COUNTESS DI LEONATI.

MISS CHISHOLM, daughter of — Chisholm, Esq., of New York.

Married to

COUNT LEONATI, of Italy.

Residence: Rome.

MRS. JOHN LESLIE.

Miss Leonie Blanche Jerome, daughter of Leonard Jerome, Esq., of New York.

Born 1866.

Married, in 1884, to

Lieutenant John Leslie, of the Grenadier Guards; served in the Egyptian Campaign; born 1857; eldest son and heir of Sir John Leslie, of Glasslough, County Monaghan, first Baronet.

Issue:

John Randolph, born 1885.

Norman Jerome, born 1886.

Residence: 11 Stratford Place, London W.

Mrs. Leslie is a sister of Lady Randolph Churchill.

BARONESS LEPELTIER-D'AUNAY.

Miss Berdan, daughter of General Berdan, U. S. A., of rifle fame.

Married to

Baron Lepeltier-d'Aunay, formerly of the French Army.

Residence: Boulevard St. Germain, Paris.

MRS. LE STRANGE.

MISS EMMELINE AUSTIN, daughter of William Austin, Esq., of Boston, Mass.

Born 1846.

Married, in 1866, to

HAMON LE STRANGE, Esq., Justice of the Peace and Deputy Lieutenant of the County of Norfolk, of which he has also held the office of High Sheriff; was formerly in the Diplomatic Service; born 1840; son of the late Henry Styleman Le Strange.

Residence: 1 Eaton Place, London S. W.

Country seat: Hunstanton Hall, Kings Lynn.

MRS. GEORGE COLLINGS LEVEY.

MRS. J. P. BOULIGNY, widow of the Hon. J. P. Bouligny, member of Congress for New Orleans, and formerly Miss Mary Elizabeth Parker, daughter of George Parker, Esq., of Washington.

Born 1848.

Married, in 1876, to

GEORGE COLLINGS LEVEY, Esq., born 1835. Australian Commissioner to the Centennial Exhibition in Philadelphia.

Created Companion of the Order of St. Michael and St. George in 1878.

MRS. NAYLOR LEYLAND.

Miss Jennie Chamberlain, daughter of P. Chamberlain, Esq., of Cleveland, O.

Born 1865.

Married, in 1889, to

Captain Herbert Naylor Leyland, Justice of the Peace and Deputy Lieutenant of Denbighshire; Captain of the Regiment of Second Life Guards; born 1864; eldest son of the late Colonel Tom Naylor Leyland.

Residence: Hyde Park House, Albert Gate, London.

Country seat: Nantclwyd Ruthin.

COUNTESS VON LINDEN.

Miss Isabella Andrews, daughter of the late Loring Andrews, Esq., who was distinguished for his generosity to the charitable institutions of New York.

Born 1854.

Married, December 2, 1876, at Stuttgart, to

His Excellency Count Eberhard von Linden, Envoy Extraordinary and Minister Plenipotentiary of the Kingdom of Wurtemburg at St. Petersburg, Chamberlain to the King of Wurtemberg; born 1836.

Residence: Wurtemberg Legation, St. Petersburg.

MME. LINDENKRONE DE HEGERMANN.

MRS. CHARLES MOULTON, widow of Charles Moulton, Esq., of Washington, and formerly Miss Greenough, daughter of the late J. Greenough, of Boston.

Born 1845.

Married, in 1886, to

His Excellency J. H. LINDENKRONE DE HEGERMANN, Envoy Extraordinary and Minister Plenipotentiary of Denmark at Rome, and a Chamberlain of His Danish Majesty.

Residence : Danish Legation, Rome.

PRINCESS DE LYNAR.

MISS MAY PARSONS, daughter of the Hon. George Parsons, of Elmenhurst, Ohio.

Born June 14, 1851.

Married, May 10, 1871, to the late

PRINCE ALEXANDER DE LYNAR (who died November 2, 1886), of the German Army.

Issue :

Prince Ernst (head of the family), born 1875.

Count George, 1877.

Countess Jane, born 1876.

Residence: Chateau of Lubbenau, near Ortrand, Merseburg, Prussia.

The Princes and Princesses de Lynar are entitled, by order of the King of Prussia, dated 1861, to the address of Serene Highness.

VISCOUNTESS MANDEVILLE.

MISS CONSUELA YZNAGA DEL VALLE, daughter of Senor Antonio Yznaga del Valle, of Ravenswood, Louisana.

Born 1855.

Married, in 1876, at New York, to

GEORGE VICTOR DROGO MONTAGUE, Viscount Mandeville, eldest son of the seventh Duke of Manchester, ; born June 17, 1853; is the Captain of the Third Battalion of Royal Irish Fusiliers; sat as M. P. for Huntingdonshire, June 1877 to 1880.

Issue:

William Angus Drogo, Lord Montague of Kimbolton, born 1877,

And twin daughters—the Hon. Jacqueline Montague and the Hon. Alice Montague—born 1879.

Residence: London.

Creation of Dukedom of Manchester, 1719. The first Duke was Secretary of State in the reign of George I.

DUCHESS OF MARLBOROUGH AND PRINCESS OF MINDELHEIM.

 Mrs Louis Hamersley, widow of the late Louis Hamersley, Esq., of New York, and formerly Miss Lilian Price, daughter of Joshua Price, Esq., of Troy.

Born 1850.

Married, at the City Hall, New York, by Mayor Hewett, July 2, 1888, and again in London, August 1888, to

George Charles Spencer Churchill, eighth Duke of Marlborough and Prince of the Holy Roman Empire; born 1844; succeeded in 1883; formerly Lieutenant Royal Horse Guards; married, 1869, to Lady Elbertha Hamilton, daughter of the first Duke of Abercorn, K. G., from whom he was divorced in 1883, and by whom he has male and female issue.

Residence: Carlton House Terrace, London.

Seat: Blenheim Palace, Woodstock, Oxfordshire.

Creation of Duchy, 1702; of Prince, 1704. The first Duke was the celebrated General.

MRS. FRANCIS MASSY-DAWSON.

MISS ELIZA GILMOUR, daughter of the late T. C. Gilmour, Esq., of New Orleans.

Born 185–.

Married, in 1870, to FRANCIS MASSY-DAW-SON, Esq., son of the late Massy-Dawson, Esq., and cousin of Lord Massy.

The Peerage of Massy was conferred in 1776.

MRS. HERBERT ST. JOHN-MILDMAY.

MISS SUSAN MOTLEY, daughter of the late his-torian and United States Envoy, John Lothrop Motley, Esq.

Born 186–.

Married, in 1884, to Colonel HERBERT ALEXANDER ST. JOHN-MILD-MAY, Gentleman-at-Arms to Her Majesty, Colonel of the Rifle Brigade; served in the Crimean war; born 1836; grandson of Sir Henry St. John-Mild-may, third Baronet.

Residence: St. James Palace, London.

Creation of Baronetcy, 1772.

MRS. LOUIS MOLESWORTH.

MISS JANE G. FROST, daughter of General Daniel Marsh Frost, of St. Louis.

Born 185–.

Married, in 1875, to

LOUIS WILLIAM, eldest son and heir of Sir Paul W. Molesworth, of Pencarrow, Cornwall, tenth Baronet.

The founder of the family was the well-known Crusader, Sir Walter de Molesworth.

Creation of the Baronetcy, 1689.

COUNTESS MOLTKE–HVITFELDT.

MISS ANNIE HUTTON, daughter of the late Benjamin Hutton, Esq., of Orange, New Jersey.

Born December 12, 1836.

Married, in 1860, to the late

COUNT HAROLD THEODOR KARL GREGOR OF MOLTKE-HVITFELDT, Captain of Danish Cavalry and Military Attache of the Danish Embassy at Paris; born 1838; died 1878, at Gastein, without issue.

Count Moltke-Hvitfeldt's brother is the present Danish Minister Plenipotentiary at Paris.

Residence: 13 Avenue de Bois de Boulogne, Paris.

Creation of Count, 1750.

COUNTESS OSCAR VON MOLTKE (ZU NOER).

MISS MARIE JANSEN, daughter of — Jansen, Esq., of Yorkville, U. S.

Born March 30, 1849.

Married, at Yorkville in 1869, to the late

COUNT OSCAR VON MOLTKE (ZU NOER); born July 1, 1828; died November 30, 1882.

No issue.

Residence: Copenhagen.

———

BARONESS MONCHEUR.

MISS HOLMAN, daughter of — Holman, Esq., of Baltimore Md.

Married to

BARON MONCHEUR.

———

MARQUISE DE MONTMORT.

MISS ELIZABETH CORBIN, daughter of Francis P. Corbin, Esq., of Virginia.

Born 185–.

Married, in 187–, to the

MARQUIS DE MONTMORT, formerly an officer in the French Army.

Residence: 5 Rue Masseran, Paris.

Country seat: Chateau de Montmort, Department Marne.

COMTESSE DE MONTAUBAN.

Miss Butterfield, daughter of General Butterfield, of New York, Paris, and Nice.

Born 185–.

Married, 187–, to the

Count de Montauban, formerly an officer in the French Army.

COUNTESS DE MONTHOLON.

Miss Mary Gratiot, daughter of the late J. Gratiot, of Kentucky.

Born 185–.

Married, in 1887, to

Count de Montholon, an officer in the French Army.

Residence : Rue Royale, Paris.

MARCHIONESS DE MORES ET DE MONTE-MAGGIORE.

Miss Medorah Marie Hoffmann, daughter of J. Hoffmann, Esq., banker, New York.

Born 1862.

Married, February 15, 1882, to

Antoine du Manca-Amat de Vallombrosa, Marquis de Mores et de Monte-Maggiore; born 1858; son and heir of Don Richard, Duc of Vallombrosa and of Asinara.

Residence: 5 Rue de Tilsit, Paris.

MRS. MOUNSEY.

MISS JONES, daughter of — Jones, Esq., of New York.

Born 1850.

Married, in 1875, to the late

CHARLES AUGUSTUS MOUNSEY, Her Majesty's Minister Plenipotentiary to Bogota, South America, by whom she has issue.

Residence: 51 Avenue Montaigne, Paris.

COUNTESS MOUNZELLI.

MISS KATE PARKES, daughter of — Parkes, Esq., of Brooklyn.

Married to

COUNT MOUNZELLI, of Italy.

LADY MUSGRAVE.

MISS JEANIE LUCINDA FIELD, daughter of David Dudley Field, Esq., of Gramercy Park, New York City.

Born 185–.

Married, in 1870, to the late

SIR ANTHONY MUSGRAVE, G. C. M. G.; born 1828; Governor and Commander-in-Chief of the Colony of Queensland, who died October 8, 1888, at Brisbane.

Residence: London.

LADY MURRAY.

MISS HELEN SANGER, daughter of Jerry Sanger, Esq., of Utica, N. Y.

Born 1841.

Married, in 1861, to

SIR DIGBY MURRAY, of Blackbarony, Peebleshire, eleventh Baronet; born October 1829; formerly an officer of the Royal Navy; is Hereditary Secretary for Scotland, and Professional Member of the Marine Department of the Government Board of Trade.

Issue:

John, born January, 1867.
Allan, born 1870.
Helen and Marian.

Residence: 34 Colville road, London, S. W.
Creation, 1628.

COUNTESS DE NARBONNE-LARA.

MISS CATHERINE PHALEN, daughter of James Phalen, Esq., of New York.

Born 1843.

Married, 1863, to the

COUNT DE NARBONNE-LARA, an officer in the French Army.

Residence: 23 Rue de Bassius, Paris.

MRS. MUNGO MURRAY.

Miss Annie Willing, daughter of Thomas Willing, Esq., of Philadelphia.

Born 1821.

Married, in 1841, to

Mungo Murray, Esq., Deputy-Lieutenant of the County of Perth; cousin of Sir Patrick Murray, of Ochtertyre,

Residence : Lintrose, Cuparangus, Scotland.

The Baronetcy was created in 1673.

MRS. WILSON NOBLE.

Miss Dana, daughter of the late Richard Henry Dana, Esq., author of " Two Years Before the Mast," &c., &c.

Born 1860.

Married, in 1879, to

Wilson Noble, Esq., Member of Parliament for Hastings and Deputy Lieutenant for the County of Sussex.

Residence : 52 Sloane St., London.

Country seat : Park Place, Henley-on-Thames, near London.

PRINCESS OF NOER.

(See Countess Waldersee.)

THE HON. MRS. NORTHCOTE.

 MISS EDITH LIVINGSTON FISH, daughter of the Hon. Hamilton Fish, of New York, formerly Secretary of State.

Born 1865.

Married, in 1883, to the Honorable HUGH OLIVER NORTHCOTE, fifth son of the late Earl of Iddesleigh (better known as Sir Stafford Northcote, formerly Secretary of State and Chancellor of the Exchequer, and brother of the second Earl); born 1854; educated at Eton and Germany; now in business in New York.

Issue:

A son, born 1887,
And a daughter, born 1885.

Residence: New York.

COUNTESS DE NEFFRAY.

MISS MEIGGS, daughter of General Meiggs, U. S. A., Washington.

Born 185–.

Married, in 187–, to

COMTE DE NEFFRAY, of France.

COMTESSE ORIOLA AND MARCHIONESS D'ALVITO.

MRS. BERNA, widow of the German Consul-General Berna, and formerly Miss Christ, daughter of the late George Christ, Esq., of New York.

Born in New York, April 18, 1846.

Married, December 18, 1880, to

COMTE WALDEMAR JOACHIM FRIEDRICH FREIMUND ALFONS LOBO DA SILVEIA, Marquis of Alvito, in the Kingdom of Portugal, and Count of Oriola in the Kingdom of Prussia; born August 27, 1854.

No issue.

Residence: Budesheim, near Heldenbergen, in the Grand Duchy of Hesse.

The Countess is a cousin of Mr. Stanley Mortimer, of New York.

Creation: Portuguese Count, 1653; Portuguese Marquis, 1776; Prussian Count, 1822.

SIGNORA SIMEONI PERUZZI.

MISS MARY STORY, daughter of William Story, Esq., the famous sculptor, of Rome.

Born 186–.

Married, in 188–, at Rome, to the

COMMENDATORE SIMEONI PERUZZI, Chamberlain to the King of Italy.

Residence: Rome.

BARONESS VON OVERBECK.

MISS DAHLGREN, daughter of the late Rear-Admiral Dahlgren, of the U. S. N.

Born 184–.

Married, in 186–, at Washington, to the late

BARON VON OVERBECK, formerly Austrian Consul-General at Hong Kong, who was created Baron for his services in advancing the interest of Austrian commerce in the East.

MRS. ARTHUR PAGET.

MISS MARY STEVENS, daughter of the late Paran Stevens, Esq., of New York.

Born 1856.

Married, in 1878, to

Lieutenant-Colonel ARTHUR HENRY FITZROY PAGET, of the Scots Guards, who served in the Ashantee War and the Nile Expedition; was formerly Page of Honor to the Queen; born in 1851; son of the late General Lord Alfred Paget, Chief Equerry to the Queen, and grandson of the first Marquis of Anglesey, K. G., the famous Waterloo General.

Issue:

      Albert Edward Sydney Louis, born 1879.

      Louisa Margaret.

Residence: No. 5 Halkin St., London, S. W.

(For family see " Marchioness of Anglesey.")

COUNTESS DE PIERRE.

Miss — Thorne, daughter of J. Thorne, Esq., of West Sixteenth Street, New York.

Born 1841.

Married, in 1861, to the late

Comte de Pierre, first Equerry of Napoleon III.

Residence: 12 Rue Boissy-d'Anglas.

Country seat: Chateau of Aulteaulteribe, Department Puy de Dome, France.

LADY PLAYFAIR.

Miss Edith Russell, daughter of S. H. Russell, Esq., of Boston.

Born 1855.

Married, as third wife, in 1878, to the

Right Honorable Sir Lyon Playfair, M. P., K. C. B., Privy Councilor, formerly Postmaster-General, and a distinguished Professor of Chemistry, Gentleman Usher to the late Prince Consort; born 1819.

No issue.

Residence: No. 68 Onslow Gardens, London.

LADY PLUNKETT.

 MISS MAY TEVIS MORGAN, daughter of Charles Waln Morgan, Esq., of Philadelphia.

Born 1850.

Married, at Paris in 1870, to the

Honorable SIR FRANCIS RICHARD PLUNKETT, K. C. M. G., Envoy Extraordinary and Minister Plenipotentiary to The Hague, youngest son of the ninth Earl of Fingal ; knighted 1887.

Issue :

      Nora, born 1871.

      Helen, born 1875.

Residence : British Legation, The Hague.

The family is descended from Sir Christopher Plunkett, 1403. Earldom of Fingal created 1613.

MARCHIONESS DI PORTA.

MISS FANNIE HUTTON, daughter of the late Benjamin Hutton, Esq., of Orange, New Jersey.

Born 185-.

Married, in 187-, to the

MARCHESE DI PORTA, of Rome.

PRINCESS PONIATOWSKI.

MISS CATHERINE MAUD ELIS GODDARD, daughter of Eli Goddard, Esq., of New York.

Born 1862.

Married, April 3, 1884, to

PRINCE CHARLES PONIATOWSKI, born 1862, son of Prince Stanislas Poniatowski, (Master of the Horse to the Emperor Napoleon III.) and of the Countess le Hon, heir to the family estates now held by the chief of the family, Prince Charles Poniatowski, born 1808.

Residence: Italy.

Creation: Prince of the Empire, 1850.

The family is descended from the old Lombard Counts of Torelli, who in 1569 emigrated to Poland. In 1769 Count Stanislas Poniatowski was elected King of Poland.

COUNTESS FRANCIS POURTALES.

MISS ELISE BACHMANN, daughter of Simon Bachmann, Esq.

Born 1825.

Married, November 19, 1848, to the late

COUNT FRANCIS LUDWIG POURTALES, Director of the Royal Zoological Museum of Boston, who died July 19, 1880.

Residence: Cambridge, Mass.

COUNTESS ARTHUR POURTALES.

MISS MARIE ADELE B. BEAUVAR-BOOSIER, daughter of — Beauvar-Boosier, Esq., of New Orleans.

Born 1852.

Married, May 2, 1876, as second wife, to

COUNT ARTHUR DE POURTALES (GORGIER), French Consul at Newcastle, England, born August 31, 1844; married first to the late Miss Jennie Lind Halliday, of New York, who died May 15, 1873.

Issue of the Count's first marriage:

A daughter, Marie, born 1871.

BARONESS VON RAABEN.

MISS MARY MOULTON, daughter of the late Charles Moulton, of Washington, and of his wife Mrs. Moulton, who has since been married to His Excellency Lindenkrone de Hagermann, the Danish Minister at Rome.

Born 1865.

Married, in 1886, to

BARON VON RAABEN, of Copenhagen, formerly an officer in the Danish Army.

Residence: Copenhagen.

COUNTESS JAMES POURTALES.

COUNTESS BERTHA POURTALES, daughter of the late Count Francis Pourtales, Director of the Boston Museum of Natural History.

Born 1852.

Married first to Sebastian Schlesinger, titular German Consul at Boston, 1871 (from whom she was divorced in May, 1886).

Married, August 25, 1866, at New York, to

COUNT JAMES POURTALES, proprietor of the family estates of Glumbovitz and Siegda and of Wiersebonne; born July, 1853, and son of the late Count Charles Pourtales, who was Master of the Ceremonies of the Court of Berlin.

The Pourtales possess the title of Count in Prussia, Austria, and France. The title was created in 1750 by the King of Prussia.

BARONESS ADOLPHE VON ROQUES.

MISS —— ——, widow of Colonel Frank Dubarry, of the Confederate Army, and of William G. Chandler, banker, of Mobile, Ala.

Born 18–.

Married, in 1867, to

BARON ADOLPHE VON ROQUES, of the Prussian Army.

COUNTESS OTTO POURTALES.

MISS LAURA MONTGOMERY, daughter of — Montgomery, Esq., of El Paso County, Colorado. Born 1858.

Married, August 21, 1881, at Florissant, El Paso County, Col., to

COUNT OTTO LUDWIG DE POURTALES; born October 7, 1855; son of the late Count Francis Pourtales, who was Director of the Zoological Museum in Boston.

Issue :

>   Francis, born 1883.
>   James, born 1885.
>   Otto, born 1886.

Residence : Florissant, El Paso County, Col.

Creation : French Count, 1750 : Prussian and Austrian Count, 1814.

BARONESS DE RIVIERA.

MISS ANNA BLUNT, daughter of — Blunt, Esq., of Washington.

Married to the

BARON DE RIVIERA.

DUCHESS OF CHOISEUL-PRASLIN.

MISS MARY ELIZABETH FORBES, daughter of Paul S. Forbes, Esq., of New York.

Born 1854.

Married, December 17, 1874, to

GASTON LOUIS PHILIPPE DU CHOISEUL-PRAS-LIN, Duc du Praslin; born August 7, 1834.

Issue:

Marquis Gaston du Choiseul-Praslin, born November 30, 1876.

Countess Marie, born 1878.

Count Gabriel, born 1879.

Count Nicolette, born 1881.

Count Gilbert, born 1882.

Count Claude, born 1883.

Count Hugh, born 1885.

Residence: Fauburg St. Honore, Paris.

VISCOUNTESS DE ROGER.

MISS MILTENBERGER, daughter of John Miltenberger, Esq., of New Orleans.

Married, at Paris, to the

VICOMTE ROGER, formerly of the French Army.

THE HON. MRS. BURKE-ROCHE.

MISS FRANCES WORK, daughter of F. Work, Esq., of New York.

Born 1862.

Married, in 1880, to the Hon. JAMES BOOTHBY BURKE-ROCHE, brother and heir presumptive of Lord Fermoy (second Baron); born July 28, 1852; educated at Trinity College, Cambridge.

Issue:

    Cynthia Burke-Roche, born 1884.

    Edmund Maurice Burke-Roche.

    Francis George Burke-Roche (twins), born 1885.

Residence: 71 Pont St., London.

Creation of Peerage, 1856. The first Peer was Lord-Lieutenant for the County of Cork, Ireland.

COUNTESS DE SAN CARLOS.

MISS EMILY O'SULLIVAN, daughter of John O'Sullivan, Esq., formerly United States Minister to Portugal.

Born 185–.

Married, in 187–, to the COMTE DE SAN CARLOS, of Spain.

Residence: Rue de Grenell, Paris.

THE HON. MRS. CHARLES MAULE RAMSAY.

MISS ESTELLE GARRISON, daughter of — Garrison, Esq., of New York.

Born 1866.

Married, in 1885, at New York, to the Honorable CHARLES MAULE RAMSAY, second son of the twelfth Earl of Dalhousie, and uncle and guardian of the present Earl; born 1859, formerly a Lieutenant of Royal Artillery.

Residence: Minnesota, U. S.

The Earldom of Dalhousie was created in 1633.

PRINCESS EMMANUEL RUSPOLI, AND PRINCESS OF POGGIO-SUASA.

MISS JOSEPHINE MARY CURTIS, daughter of the late Joseph D. B. Curtis, Esq., of New York.

Born 1865.

Married, at Paris, June 18, 1885, to DON EMMANUEL, Prince of Ruspoli and Prince of Poggio-Suasa (who has been twice before married, and has issue by both marriages). The Prince is Deputy in the Italian Parliament, and was born in 1838.

Residence: 18 Rue Marboeuf, Paris.

Country seat: Chateau de Romaine, Lesigny, Department Seine et Marne.

PRINCESS ALEXANDER RUSPOLI.

Miss Eva Broadwood, daughter of Thomas Capel Broadwood, Esq., of New York.

Born 1859.

Married, in October, 1877, to

Don Alexander, Prince of Ruspoli, Lieutenant of Italian Cavalry and Knight of the Order of Malta; born 1844; is a brother of the head of the House of Ruspoli.

Issue:

> Don Fabrice, born December, 1878.
>
> Don Sporza, born June, 1882.
>
> Don Napoleon, born November, 1885.

Residence: Rome.

The head of the family, Don Francis, Prince of Ruspoli, is Hereditary Grand Chamberlain of His Holiness the Pope. The family is related to the Bonapartes, and is one of the most ancient of the Italian nobility.

COUNTESS SANZA DE LOBO.

Miss Allen, daughter of John Allen, Esq., of New York.

Married to

Count Sanza de Lobo, of Portugal

THE HON. MRS. SANDYS.

MISS MARIA IDA JONES, daughter of W. F. Jones, Esq., formerly of New York, now of Rio Janeiro.

Born 1862.

Married, in 1884, to the Honorable EDMUND ARTHUR MARCUS SANDYS, fourth son of the late Lord Sandys, third Baron, and brother of the present Peer; born 1860.

Residence: 32 St. Leonard's Terrace, Chelsea.

Country seat: The Vine, Thorpe, Chertsey, near London.

MARQUISE DE SAN MARZANO.

MISS GILLENDER, daughter of the late millionaire tobacconist, Eccles Gillender, Esq., of New York.

Born 185–.

Married, in 187–, to the

MARQUIS DE SAN MARZANO, of Italy.

The Marchioness is separated from her husband. When Mrs. Gillender, her mother, died in 1888, she left a will disinheriting her daughter, and leaving her entire fortune to her titled son-in-law. The Marchioness is contesting the will. (See N. Y. City records.)

COUNTESS DE SARTIGES.

Miss Ella Thorndike, daughter of W. Thorndike, Esq., of New York.

Born 185–.

Married, at Paris, in 187–, to

Count de Sartiges, former Ambassador in the French Diplomatic Service; Grand Cross of the Legion of Honor; born 1850.

Residence: 16 Rue de l'Elysee, Paris.

Country seat: Cannes.

———

MRS. ALGERNON SARTORIS.

Miss Nellie Grant, daughter of the late General Ulysses S. Grant, U. S. A., twice President of the United States.

Born 1855.

Married, at the White House, Washington, D. C., May 21, 1874, to

Algernon Sartoris, Esq., Deputy Lieutenant of Carmarthenshire; son of the late Edward Sartoris, Esq., M. P., of Warnford Park, Hants, and his wife Adelaide Kemble, sister of the celebrated Fannie Kemble; born 1851.

Residence: Warsash House, Hants, England, and Llanganneck Park, Llanelly.

PRINCESS LOUIS DE SCEY-MONTBELIARD.

Miss Winnaretta Singer, daughter of the late Isaac Singer, Esq., of Boston, of sewing-machine fame.

Born 1863.

Married, in 1887, at Paris, to

Prince Louis de Scey-Montbeliard, formerly an officer in the French Army.

Residence: 47 Rue de Sablons, Paris.

Country seat: Chateau de Scey-Le-Chatel, Department Doubes.

———

MRS. ARTHUR SMITH-BARRY.

Mrs. Arthur Post, widow of the late Arthur Post, Esq., of New York, and formerly Miss Mary Wadsworth, daughter of the late General Wadsworth, of Genesee County, N. Y., of the United States Army, War Governor of Washington.

Born 185–.

Married, in 1889, to

Arthur Smith-Barry, Esq., M. P., Deputy-Lieutenant for the County of Cheshire; has been High Sheriff of the County; born 1843. Married, first, Lady Mary, daughter of the third Earl of Dunraven, who died in 1884.

Residence: 23 Wilton Crescent, London.

Country seat: Marbury Hall, Cheshire.

MME. VON SCHWEINITZ.

Miss Jay, daughter of John Jay, Esq., of New York, formerly United States Minister to Vienna. Born 1855.

Married, in 1874, to

His Excellency General Von Schweinitz, German Ambassador at St. Petersburg, and Aide-de-Camp General to the Emperor of Germany.

Issue: numerous.

Residence: German Embassy, St. Petersburg.

BARONESS SEYDLITZ.

Miss Cornelia Roosevelt, daughter of the late Charles Roosevelt, Esq., of New York, and granddaughter of the well-known judge of that name.

Born 1867.

Married, 1888, at New York, to

Baron G. Seydlitz, Lieutenant of the Prussian Cavalry; born 1851.

Residence: Berlin.

The family of Seydlitz is one of the most ancient and famous in Prussia. One of the members was a celebrated cavalry general of Frederick the Great.

BARONESS VON SCHROEDER.

Miss Donohue, daughter of — Donohue, Esq., of San Francisco.

Born 1850.

Married to the

Baron Von Schroeder, of Germany.

COUNTESS DE SERES.

Miss Mary Niven, daughter of the late Robert Niven, Esq., of New York, and step-daughter of Mrs. Robert Niven, who is the daughter of the late Commodore Vanderbilt.

Born 1865.

Married, 1887, to the

Comte de Seres, an officer in the French Army, and eldest son and heir of the Marquis de Seres, of the Chateau de Madon, Department Loire et Cher.

Residence: 41 Rue Pierre Charron, Paris.

COUNTESS SODERINI.

Miss Stokes, daughter of J. Stokes, Esq., of Philadelphia.

Married to

Count Soderini, of Italy, Chamberlain to His Holiness the Pope.

MRS. ALGERNON BRINSLEY SHERIDAN.

MISS MARY L. MOTLEY, daughter of the late John Lothrop Motley, Esq., former United States Minister to Vienna.

Born 1850.

Married, in 1871, to

ALGERNON BRINSLEY SHERIDAN, Justice of the Peace and Deputy-Lieutenant of the County of Dorset, England; born 1845; formerly an officer in the Royal Navy; son of the late R. B. Sheridan, Esq., M. P.

Country seat: Frampton Court, Dorsetshire.

BARONESS LUDWIG VON STEIN.

MISS ANNA FORSTER, daughter of — Forster, Esq., of Brooklyn.

Born 1846.

Married, January 1871, at Brooklyn, to

BARON LUDWIG ADOLPHUS VON STEIN, of Prussia; born 1843.

Issue:

Baron Charles, born 1871.
Baron Louis, born 1874.
Baroness Mary, born 1876.

Residence: Brooklyn, N. Y.

COUNTESS DE SAINT ROMAN.

MISS SLIDELL, daughter of the late — Slidell, Esq., of Virginia.

Born 184–.

Married, in 186–, to the

COMTE DE SAINT ROMAN, of Paris.

Residence: 20 Rue Taitbout, Paris.

Country seat: Chateau de Gouvieux, Department Oise, France.

BARONESS FRANZ STILLFRIED.

MISS ELIZABETH CHIZELLE, daughter of — Chizelle, Esq., of Philadelphia.

Born 1842.

Married, in 1875, to

BARON FRANZ DE PAULO STILLFRIED; born 1837.

Residence: Rattonitz, Germany.

Creation of title, 1499.

PRINCESS DE SUZANET.

MISS FIELD, daughter of — Field, Esq., of New York.

Married to the

PRINCE DE SUZANET, of France, formerly an officer of the French Army.

Residence: Paris.

MME. A. L. E. DE STUERS.

MISS ELIZABETH CAREY, daughter of J. Carey, Esq., of New York, and niece of Mrs. W. Astor, of New York.

Born 186–.

Married, in 188–, to

His Excellency the Chevalier A. L. E. DE STUERS, Envoy Extraordinary and Minister Plenipotentiary of the King of the Netherlands, at Paris.

Residence: Dutch Legation, Rue la Perouse, Paris.

MARQUISE DE TALLYRAND-PERIGORD.
(Divorced.)

MISS BESSIE CURTIS, daughter of Joseph D. B. Curtis, Esq., of New York.

Born 1849.

Married, March 18, 1867, at Nice, to the

MARQUIS MAURICE DE TALLYRAND-PERIGORD (who since being divorced from her has become Duke of Dino); divorced August 11, 1886.

Issue:

Palma de Tallyrand-Perigord, born in Venice, April 2, 1871.

Residence: Rue St. Dominique, Paris.

The head of the family is the Duke of Sagan and Duke of Valencay.

COUNTESS TELFENER.

Miss Ada Hungerford, of California, daughter of the late — Hungerford, Esq., of California, and sister of Mrs. John W. Mackay "the Bonanza Queen."

Born 184–.

Married, 1876, to

Count Josef Telfener, President of the Royal Geographical Society at Rome.

Residence; 46 Avenue du Bois de Boulogne, Paris.

MARCHIONESS THEODOLLI.

Miss Conrad, daughter of — Conrad, Esq., of New York.

Married to the

Marquis Theodolli, of Rome.

MARQUISE DI TORRIGIANI.

Miss Fry, daughter of the late Horatio Fry, Esq., of New York, niece of the late General George B. McClellan.

Born 186–.

Married, 1885, at Rome, to the

Marquis Carlo Vetti Torrigiani, of Florence, Italy.

MARCHIONESS DE TIFFINI.

MISS WICKERSHAW, daughter of — Wickershaw, Esq., of New York.

Married to the

MARQUIS DE TIFFINI, of Italy.

MRS. TREMENHEERE.

MISS JESSIE VAN AUKEN, daughter of William B. Van Auken, Esq., of Fifth avenue, New York.

Born 1869.

Married, October 18, 1887, at New York, to

HENRY TREMENHEERE, Esq., Magistrate in the Madras Civil Service; son of Lieutenant-General C. W. Tremenheere, C. B., formerly Military Governor of Aden.

COUNTESS DE TROBRIAND.

MISS MARY JONES, daughter of — Jones, Esq., of New York.

Born 182–.

Married, 186–, to the

COUNT DE TROBRIAND, of France, formerly a General in the United States Army.

Residence: 47 Avenue des Champs Elysees, Paris.

COUNTESS DE LA TORRE.

Miss HAIGHT, daughter of — Haight, Esq., of New York.

Married to

COUNT DE LA TORRE, of Spain.

———

MARQUISE DE VALORI.

Miss MARY LEDOUX, daughter of J. Ledoux, Esq., New Orleans.

Born 185–.

Married, 188–, to

MARQUIS DE VALORI, of France, formerly an officer in the French Army.

Residence: 15 Rue Vernet, Paris.

———

THE HON. MRS. VERNON.

Miss LOUISE FROST, daughter of — Frost, Esq., of St. Louis, U. S.

Born 186–.

Married, 1884, to the

Honorable WILLIAM FREDERICK CUTHBERT VERNON; born July 18, 1856; heir presumptive to the Barony of his brother, Lord Vernon.

Issue:

Richard Henry, born 1885.

LADY VERNON.

Miss Frances Margaret Lawrence, daughter of Francis Lawrence, Esq., of New York.

Born 1865.

Married, 1885, to

George William Venables Vernon, Lord Vernon, seventh Baron; born February 25, 1854; formerly Captain Twelfth Lancers; Justice of the Peace for Derbyshire.

Issue:

Fannie Lawrence Venables Vernon, born 1866.

Residence: 38 Hill St., Berkeley Square, London.

Seats: Sudbury Hall, Derby; Poynton Hall, Stockford.

Creation of title, 1762. The first Lord was M. P. for Litchfield.

DUCHESS OF VILLARS-BLANCA.

Miss Mary Schenck, a niece of General Robert C. Schenck, formerly Minister to England, and Member of Congress.

Born 1846.

Married, 1886, to the

Duke of Villars-Blanca, of Spain; a Grandee of the First-Class, and formerly an officer in the Spanish Army.

Residence: Madrid.

MRS. HARCOURT VERNON.

Miss Helen Rebecca Traer, daughter of J. W. Traer, Esq., of Cedar Rapids, Iowa, U. S.

Born 1866.

Married, 1884, to

Walther Granville Harcourt Vernon, formerly Lieutenant Derbyshire Regiment; born 1860; son of the Rev. Evelyn Harcourt Vernon.

Belongs to the family of Lord Vernon.

COUNTESS FOLCHI-VICI.

Miss McAllister, daughter of — McAllister, Esq., of Philadelphia.

Married, 1880, in London, by Cardinal Manning, to

Count Guiseppe Folchi-Vici, of Italy.

BARONESS PAUL VIETINGHOFF.

Miss Louise Friedner, daughter of — Friedner, Esq., of San Francisco.

Born 1866.

Married, at New York, October 9, 1887, to

Baron Paul Vietinghoff, of Russia.

Creation of title, 1818.

Residence: New York.

PRINCESS VICOVARO.

MISS ELEANOR SPENCER, daughter of Lorillard Spencer, Esq., of New York.

Born, January 7, 1851.

Married, June 25, 1870, to

DON VIRGINIUS CENCI, sixth Prince of Vicovaro, Count Palatine, and Knight of the Order of Malta ; born August 16, 1840 ; also Marquis of Roccapriora.

Issue :

> Donna Eleanor, born 1875.
>
> Donna Beatrix, born 1877.

Residence : The Cenci Palace, Rome.

Creation of Prince, 1692. The family traces its ancestry in direct line back to Marco Cincio, who was Prefect of Pisa in the year 457. John Cenci was Pope under the name of John X. A. D. 914.

Princess Vicovaro is Lady in Waiting to Queen Marguerite, of Italy.

BARONESS VILAIN XIV.

MISS EMILY GORDON, daughter of the late J. Gordon, of Ohio.

Born 1862.

Married, 1884, to

BARON VILAIN XIV., formerly an officer in the Belgian cavalry.

Residence: Brussels.

The Vilains are one of the oldest families of Belgium, and are distinguished by their various numerals.

MRS. WADDINGTON.

MISS KING, daughter of Charles King, Esq., of New York, formerly President of Columbia College.

Born 184-.

Married, 186-, at Paris, to

His Excellency, WILLIAM HENRY WADDINGTON, French Ambassador to the Court of St. James, and formerly French Minister of Foreign Affairs; a member of the Senate and the Institute.

Residence: French Embassy, Albert Gate House, Hyde Park, London, and 31 Rue Dumont d'Urville, Paris.

MRS. ROBERT HORACE WALPOLE.

 Miss Louise Corbin, daughter of Daniel C. Corbin, Esq., of New York, and niece of Austin Corbin, Esq. Born 1867.

Married, in 1888, to CAPTAIN ROBERT HORACE WALPOLE, formerly of the Royal Navy; Captain of Militia, nephew and heir of the fourth Earl of Orford, born 1854.

Residence : 4 Dean street, Park Lane, London. County Seat: Weybourne Holt, Norfolk.

Creation of the Earldom, 1806; creation of the Barony of Walpole, 1726.

The founder of the family was Sir Robert Walpole, Prime Minister of England and K. G., 1726.

MRS. WESTENBERG.

Miss Mary King, daughter of Charles King, Esq., formerly President of Columbia College, and sister of Mrs. Waddington, the French Ambassadress in London.

Born 1848.

Married, 188–, to His Excellency,

B. O. T. H. WESTENBERG, Envoy Extraordinary and Minister Plenipotentiary of the King of the Netherlands at Rome.

Residence : Dutch Legation, Rome.

COUNTESS VON WALDERSEE, PRINCESS OF NOER.

PRINCESS FREDERICK, widow of Prince Frederick of Schleswig-Holstein-Sonderburg-Augustenburg, who was created Prince of Noer by the Emperor of Austria on the 28th of September, 1864, and who died at Bayreuth, Syria, July, 1865; and formerly Miss Mary Esther Lee, daughter of the late David Lee, Esq., of New York.

Born, October 3, 1838.

Married, April 14, 1874, to General Alfred, Count Waldersee, Aide-de-camp-General to the Emperor of Germany, Chief of the General Staff of the German Army, Chevalier of Justice of the Order of St. John, born April, 1832.

Residence: Berlin.

———

PRINCESS YTURBIDE.

MISS JOSEPHINE GREENE, daughter of — Greene, Esq., of Georgetown, and granddaughter of the Colonial Governor of Maryland.

Married to the late

PRINCE ANGEL DE YTURBIDE, the adopted son and heir of the late Emperor Maximilian of Mexico, by whom she has issue.

LADY WATERLOW.

MISS MARGARET HAMILTON, daughter of the late William Hamilton, Esq., of Napa, Cal.

Born 1860.

Married, as second wife, in 1882, to

SIR SIDNEY HEDLEY WATERLOW, first Baronet, formerly Lord Mayor of London, Governor of the Bank of England, Chairman of the London, Chatham, and Dover R. R., Member of Parliament, and an Alderman for the City of London; born 1822.

Issue by first marriage.

Residence: 29 Chesham Place, London, S. W.

Seat: Trosley Towers, Wrotham, Seven Oaks, Kent.

Creation of title, 1873.

MARCHIONESS D'YRUJO.

MISS McKEENE, daughter of — McKeene, Esq., of Philadelphia.

Married to the

MARQUIS D'YRUJO, of Spain.

LADY WOLSELEY.

Miss Anita Theresa Murphy, daughter of the late Daniel T. Murphy, Esq., of San Francisco.

Born 1865.

Married, in 1883, to

Sir Charles Michael Wolseley, Staffordshire, ninth Baronet; born 1846; Justice of Peace, and Deputy-Lieutenant for the County of Stafford.

Seat: Wolseley Hall, Rugeley, Staffordshire.

Creation of title, 1628.

This ancient Staffordshire family traces its descent back to the year 1281.

THE ROYAL FAMILY.

REIGNING SOVEREIGN.

VICTORIA, Queen of the United Kingdom of Great Britain and Ireland, Empress of India.

Her Majesty ALEXANDRINA VICTORIA, only child of F. M., H. R. H., Prince Edward Duke of Kent and Strathearne, who died 1820 (Fourth son of King George III.), and of H. S. H. Victoria Mary Louisa, who died in 1861, widow of H. S. H. Charles Louis, Prince of Leiningen, and daughter of H. S. H. Francis, Duke of Saxe-Coburg-Saalfield.

Born May 24th, 1819.

Ascended the throne on the decease of her uncle, King William IV., on June 20th, 1837.

Crowned in Westminister Abbey, June 28th, 1838.

THE ROYAL FAMILY.

Proclaimed Empress of India at Delhi, January 1st, 1877.

Married at St. James' Palace, February 10th, 1840, H. R. H. PRINCE FRANCIS ALBERT AUGUSTUS CHARLES EMMANUEL, Duke of Saxony, and Prince of Saxe-Coburg and Gotha, created " His Royal Highness " February 7th, 1840, and "Prince Consort" June 25th, 1857, who died December 14th, 1861, second son of Ernest Frederick Anthony Charles Louis, late reigning Duke of Saxe-Coburg and Gotha, and has issue.

SONS LIVING.

Albert Edward (Prince of Wales).

Prince Alfred Ernest Albert (Duke of Edinburgh).

Prince Arthur William Patrick Albert (Duke of Connaught and Strathearne).

DAUGHTERS LIVING.

Princess Victoria Adelaide Mary Louisa (Crown Princess of Germany and Prussia), Princess Royal of England, Duchess of Saxony.

Born November 21st, 1840.

Granted, by Act of Parliament, a dower of £40,000, and an annuity of £8,000 a year.

Is a Member of the Royal Order of Victoria and Albert (1st Class), and a Lady of the Imperial Order of the Crown of India, and of the Royal Red Cross, &c.

Married, January 25th, 1858, H. I. H. Prince Frederick William Nicholas Charles, K. G., G. C. B., Crown Prince of Germany and Prussia, only son of H. I. M. William, Emperor of Germany and King of Prussia, and has issue:

Sons Living : Prince Frederick William Victor Albert, K. G.

Born Jan. 27th, 1859.

Created a K. G. by Patent 1877.

Married, Feb. 27th, 1881, Augusta Victoria Amelia Louise Maria Constance (born Oct. 22d, 1858), eldest daughter of Frederic, Grand Duke of Schleswig-Holstein - Sonderburg - Augustenburg, and has issue living.

Prince Frederic Wilhelm Victor August Ernst, born May 6th, 1882.

Prince Wilhelm Eitel Friedrich Christian Karl, born July 7th, 1883.

Prince Adalbert Ferdinand Berengar Victor, born July 14th, 1884.

Prince August William Henry

THE ROYAL FAMILY.

Gunther Victor, born Jan. 29th, 1887.

Residence : Berlin.

Prince Albert William Henry, G. C. B., born August 14th, 1862.

Daughters Living : Princess Victoria Elizabeth Augusta Charlotte (Hereditary Princess of Saxe Meiningen), born July 24th, 1860, married Feb. 18th, 1878, Bernard, Hereditary Prince of Saxe Meiningen, and has issue living.

Princess Feodora Victoria Augusta Marianna Maria, born May 13th, 1879.

Princess Frederika Wilhelmina Amelia Victoria, born April 12th, 1866.

Princess Sophia Dorothea Ulirke Alice, born June 14th, 1870.

Princess Margaret Beatrice Feodora, born April 22d, 1872.

Residences : Berlin, The New Palace, Potsdam.

THE ROYAL FAMILY.

 Princess Helena Augusta Victoria (Princess Christian), Duchess of Saxony.

Born May 25th, 1846.

Granted by Act of Parliament, in Feb. 1866, a dower of £30,000 and an annuity of £6,000.

Received, 1874, Russian Order St. Catherine.

Is a Member of the Royal Order of Victoria and Albert (1st class), and a Lady of the Imperial Order of the Crown of India, and of the Royal Red Cross, &c.

Married, July 5th, 1866, H. R. H. Prince Frederick Christian Charles Augustus of Schleswig-Holstein, K. G. Prince Christian was granted the title of Royal Highness June 30th, 1866, and is a General in British Army, High Steward at Windsor, and a Bencher of the Inner Temple, and has isssue.

Sons Living: Prince Christian Victor Albert Ludwig Ernst Anton, born April 14th, 1867, educated at Wellington College, at Magdalen College, Oxford, and Royal Military College, Sandhurst.

Prince Albert John Charles Frederick Alfred George, born Feb. 26th, 1869, educated at Charterhouse.

THE ROYAL FAMILY.

Daughters Living: Princess Victoria Louise Sophia Augusta Amelia Helena, born May 3d, 1870.

Princess Franziska Josepha Louise Augusta Marie Christiana Helena, born Aug. 12, 1872.

By Royal warrant the children of Prince and Princess Christian are to hold and enjoy the title, and attribute, of " Highness " prefixed to their Christian names, or any titles of honor which may belong to them.

Residence : Cumberland Lodge, Windsor Park.

 Princess Louise Caroline Alberta (Princess Louise, Marchioness of Lorne), Duchess of Saxony.

Born March 18th, 1848.

Granted by Act of Parliament, Feb. 1871, a dower of £30,000 and an annuity of £6,000.

Received, 1874, Russian Order St. Catherine.

Is a Member of the Royal Order Victoria and Albert (1st class), and a Lady of the Imperial Crown of India and of the Royal Red Cross, &c.

Married, March 21st, 1871, the Marquis of Lorne, P. C., K. T. G. C. M. G., formerly Governor-General of Canada, eldest son of 8th Duke of Argyll.

Residence : Kensington Palace, W.

THE ROYAL FAMILY.

 Princess Beatrice Mary
Victoria Feodore (Prin-
cess Beatrice), Duchess of Saxony.

Born April 14th, 1857. Is a Member of the
Royal Order of Victoria and Albert (1st class),
and a Lady of the Order of the Imperial Crown of
India, and of the Royal Red Cross, &c.

Received, 1874, Russian Order St. Catherine.

Is a Dame Chevaliere of St. John of Jerusalem.

Granted by Act of Parliament, July, 1885, a
dower of £30,000 and an annuity of £6,000.

Married, July 23d, 1885, H. R. H. Prince Henry
Maurice of Battenberg, K. G. (Colonel Isle of
Wight Rifle Volunteers). Prince Henry of Bat-
tenberg was granted the title of Royal Highness
July 22nd, 1885, and was naturalized by Act of
Parliament, August 1885. He is the third son of
Prince Alexander of Hesse, G. C. B., and has is-
sue living:

Son Living: Prince Albert Alexander, born
November 23d, 1886.

Daughter Living: Princess Victoria Eugenie
Julia Ena, born October 24th, 1887.

The title of " Highness " was, on December
13th, 1886, granted to Prince Albert Alexander
and to any other children that might be born
to their Royal Highnesses.

Residence: Windsor Castle.

THE ROYAL FAMILY.

Issue of H. R. H. the late Leopold George Duncan Albert, K. G., fourth son of H. M. Queen Victoria.

See Duke of Albany.

Issue of the late Princess Alice Maud Mary (Grand Duchess of Hesse), Duchess of Saxony, second daughter of H. M. the Queen. She was born April 25th, 1843; married July 1st, 1862, Louis IV., reigning Grand Duke of Hesse, K. G., and died December 14th, 1878:

Prince Ernest Louis Charles Albert William (Hereditary Grand Duke of Hesse), born November 25th, 1868.

Princess Victoria Alberta Elizabeth Matilda Mary, born April 5th, 1863; married April 30th, 1884, H. S. H. Prince Louis Alexander of Battenberg, G. C. B., Com. R. N., and has issue living:

Princess Victoria Alice Elizabeth Julia Marie, born March, 1885.

Princess Elizabeth Alexandrina Louisa Alice, born November 1st 1864; married, 1884, the Grand Duke Serge of Russia.

Princess Irene Marie Louisa Anna, born July 11th, 1866.

Princess Victoria Alice Helena Louise Beatrice, born June 6th, 1872.

PALACES.—Windsor Castle, Berkshire; Os-

THE ROYAL FAMILY.

borne House, Isle of Wight; Balmoral, Scotland; Buckingham Palace, S. W.

PRINCE OF WALES.

F. M., His Royal Highness Albert Edward, K. G., P. C., K. T., K. P., G. C. B., G. C. S. I., G. C. M. G., G. C. I. E., D. C. L., LL. D., Mus. D., Prince of Wales and Earl of Chester, Earl of Dublin, Prince of Great Britain and Ireland, Duke of Saxony, Prince of Coburg and Gotha, Duke of Cornwall, and Duke of Rothsay, Earl of Carrick, Baron of Renfrew, Lord of the Isles, and Great Steward of Scotland.

Born November 9th, 1841.

Educated at Ch. Ch., Oxford, and at Trinity College Cambridge, (D. C. L. of Oxford 1868, LL. D. of Cambridge, and of Trinity College, Dublin, 1868, LL. D. of Calcutta University 1875, and Mus. D. of Royal University of Ireland 1885); Bencher of the Middle Temple 1861, and Treasurer 1887; appointed a Colonel in the Army 1858, a General 1862, and a Field Marshal 1875; is Colonel in Ch. of 1st and 2d Life Guards and of Royal Horse Guards, Colonel 10th Hussars, Captain-General and Colonel Honorable Artillery of London, Honorable Colonel of 2d Brigade E. Division R. A., of 3d Batallion Duke of Cornwall's L. I., of 3d Batallion Gordon Highlanders, of 4th Volunteer Batallion Suffolk Regiment (Cambridge University Volunteers), of 1st Volunteer Batallion Oxfordshire L. I., of 6th Volunteeer Batallion King's Royal Rifle Corps, of 2d Volunteer Batallion Seaforth Highlanders (Ross-shire Buffs, the Duke of Albany's), of 2nd Regiment of Goorka Infantry, of 6th Bengal Cavalry, of Ceylon L. I. Volunteers, and of Pomera-

THE ROYAL FAMILY.

nian (Blucher) Hussars, and a Field Marshal in
the Prussian Army; was Colonel in Ch. of Rifle
Brigade 1868-80; elected an Elder Brother of
Trinity House 1869; installed Grand Master of
Freemasons in England 1874; is a Governor of
Charterhouse and of Christ's Hospital, President
of Society of Arts, and of St. Bartholomew's Hospital, and a High Steward of Plymouth, &c.; introduced at Privy Council 1863, and at Privy
Council in Ireland 1868; granted in 1863, by
Act of Parliament, an annuity of £40,000 a year,
exclusive of the Revenues of the Duchy of Corn-
wall; appointed a Personal A. D. C. to H. M.
1876, and Honorable Admiral of the Fleet 1887;
has Orders of Elephant of Denmark, Black Eagle
of Prussia, St. John of Germany, Tower and
Sword of Portugal, St. Stephen of Austria, Southern Cross of Brazil, Golden Fleece of Spain, Grand
Cross of the Legion of Honor of France, and
Charles III. of Spain, and Grand Order of the
Chrysanthemum of Japan, &c.

Married, March 10th, 1863, the Princess Alex-
andria Caroline Mary Charlotte Louisa Julia of
Denmark (born December 1st, 1844), eldest daughter of Christian IX., King of Denmark, and has
issue.

Patron of twenty-one livings: Calstock R.,
Davidstow V., Landulph R., Lanteglos R., Mi-

chaelstow R., St. Burian R., St. Levan R., Sennen R., Stoke Climsland R., Stratton V. and Treneglos V., Cornwall ; Curry Mallet R., West Harptree V., Ile Brewers V., and Stratton-on-the-Foss R., Somerset; Lydford R., Devon ; Ryme Intrinseca R., Dorset; Northchurch R., Herts; Sandingham R., W. Newton R., Norfolk; and alternately of Shepton Mallet R., Somerset.

SEAT: Sandringham, Norfolk.

TOWN MANSION: Marlborough House, Pall Mall, S. W.

CLUBS: United Service, Travelers', Army and Navy, Guards', Marlborough, Junior Naval and Military, United University, Turf, Yorkshire, Hurlingham.

SONS LIVING.

Prince Albert Victor Christian Edward K. G., K. P.

Born January 8th, 1864.

Educated at Cambridge University, Honorable LL. D., Dublin, 1887.

Appointed a Naval Cadet 1877, a Midshipman R. N. 1879; Honorable Lieutenant R. N. Reserve 1883, and Lieutenant 2d Brigade E. Division R. A. 1885, when he was transferred to the 10th Hussars, of which Regiment he is Captain; is attached for duty to the 9th Lancers; is a Personal A. D. C. to H. M. ; elected a Bencher of the Mid-

THE ROYAL FAMILY.

dle Temple January 21st, 1885 ; has Orders of the
Black Eagle of Prussia, Grand Gordon Osmanie
of Turkey, Collar of Charles III. of Spain, Grand
Cross of Netherlands Lion, Insignia of Annun-
ciata of Italy, and Star of Roumania, &c.

CLUBS: Marlborough, Junior Naval and Military.

Prince George Frederick
Ernest Albert, K. G., born
June 3d, 1865.

Became a Naval Cadet 1877, a Midshipman
1879, a Sub-Lieutenant 1884, and Lieutenant 1885;
is a Personal Naval A. D. C. to H. M.; has Grand
Gordon Order of Osmanie of Turkey.

CLUBS : Marlborough, Junior Naval and Military.

DAUGHTERS LIVING,

Princess Louise Victoria Alexandra Dagmar,
born February 20th, 1867.

Is a Lady of the Imperial Order of the Crown
of India.

Princess Victoria Alexandra Olga Mary, born
July 6th, 1868.

Is a Lady of the Imperial Order of the Crown
of India.

Princess Maud Charlotte Mary Victoria, born
November 26th, 1869.

THE ROYAL FAMILY.

DUKE OF EDINBURGH.

His Royal Highness Alfred Ernest Albert, K. G., P. C., K. T., K. P., G. C. M. G., G. C. S. I., G. C. I. E., LL. D., 1st Duke, Duke of Saxony, Prince of Saxe-Coburg-Gotha.

Born August 6th, 1844.

Educated at Bonn, and at University of Edinburgh (Honorable LL. D. 18—, D. C. L., Oxford, 1887); entered R. N. August 1858, became Lieutenant 1863, Captain 1866, Rear-Admiral 1879, and Admiral 1887; commanded the Galatea 1867–72, the Sultan 1876–8, the Black Prince 1878, and the Channel Squadron 1883–4; elected King of Greece, December 1862, but declined the dignity; elected Master of Trinity House, March 15th, 1866; created Duke of Edinburg, Earl of Ulster, and Earl of Kent (in peerage of United Kingdom), 1866; introduced to Privy Council, May 9th, 1866; was Colonel 1st London Artillery Volunteers 1868-75; has been Honorable Colonel 3d Brigade Scottish Division R. A. since 1874, of the Royal Marines since 1882, and of 3d Batallion Black Watch (Royal Highlanders); was some time Admiral Sup. of Naval Reserves; appointed a Personal Naval A. D. C. to H. M. 1876; has been Commander-in-Chief of Mediterranean Fleet since 1886; has Orders of Tower and Sword of Portugal,

THE ROYAL FAMILY.

Black Eagle of Prussia, the Elephant of Denmark, and the Star of the Osmanie of Turkey in brilliants, &c. ; in 1866 was granted, by Act of Parliament, an annuity of £15,000, and in 1874 an additional £10,000; is h.-p. to Grand Duke of Saxe-Coburg-Gotha, a Colonel in German Army, and Captain in Russian Black Sea Fleet, &c.

Married, January 23d, 1874, the Grand Duchess Marie Alexandrovna, born October 17th, 1853, only daughter of H. M. the Emperor of All the Russias, and has issue.

TOWN RESIDENCE : Clarence House, St. James', S. W.

CLUBS: United Service, White's, Travelers', Army and Navy, Junior United Service, Marlborough, Junior Naval and Military, University (Edinburgh), Hurlingham.

SON LIVING.

Prince Alfred Alexander Ernest William Albert, Earl of Ulster, born October 15th, 1874.

DAUGHTERS LIVING.

Princess Marie Alexandra Victoria, born October 1875.

Princess Victoria Melita, born November 9th, 1876.

Princess Alexandra Louise Olga Victoria, born September 1st, 1878.

THE ROYAL FAMILY.

Princess Beatrice Leopoldine Victoria, born April 20th, 1884.

DUKE OF CONNAUGHT AND STRATHEARNE.

His Royal Highness Arthur William Patrick Albert, K. G., P. C., K. T., K. P., G. C. S. I., G. C. M. G., G. C. I. E., C. B., 1st Duke, Duke of Saxony, Prince of Saxe-Coburg-Gotha.

Born May 1st, 1850.

Educated at Royal Military Academy, Woolwich; D. C. L., Oxford, 1887; appointed Lieutenant R. E. 1868, transferred to R. A. October 1868, and to Rifle Brigade August 1869; became Captain 1871, transferred to 7th Hussars 1874, promoted to Major 1875, transferred as Lieutenant-Colonel to command 1st Batallion Rifle Brigade 1876, promoted Brevet-Colonel and Major-General 1880, appointed Colonel in Ch. of Rifle Brigade (Prince Consort's Own) 1880, and Colonel Scots Guards 1883, was Brigadier-General in command 3d Infantry Brigade at Aldershot 1880–82, commanded 1st Brigade 1st Division of Egyptian Expeditionary Force 1882 (medal with clasp, Grand Order of Osmanie, 2d class Medjidie, C. B., and thanked by Parliament), an Infantry Brigadier at Aldershot 1883, and Meerut Division Bengal 1883–5 and 1886, since when he has been Commander in Ch. of Troops at Bombay Pres; introduced at Privy Council 1871; created Duke of Connaught and of Strathearne, and Earl of Sussex (in peerage of United Kingdom) 1874; was Hon. Colonel E. Kent Yeo. Cavalry 1873–8; is Ranger of Epping Forest, Great Prior of Ireland, a Bencher of Gray's Inn, Hon. Colonel of 3d Brigade S. Division R. A., of 3d and 4th Batallions Queen's Own (Royal W. Kent Regiment), of Royal E. Kent Yeo. Cavalry, of 4th Volunteer Batallion Rifle Brigade (Prince Consort's Own), of 13th (Duke of Connaught's) Bengal Lancers, of 7th Bengal N. I., of 29th Bombay N. I. (2d Biluch Regiment), and of Brandenburg Ziethen Regiment of Hussars, a Personal A. D. C. to H. M., and a Chevalier of Justice of Order of St. John of Jerusalem, &c.; has Orders of Black Eagle of Prussia, Elephant of Denmark, Seraphim of Sweden, St. Andrew of Russia, St. Stephen of Austria, Charles III. of Spain, and the Osmanie, &c.; granted in 1871, by Act of Parliament, an annuity of £15,000, and in 1879 an additional £10,000; Hon. Doctor of Literature of Punjab University 1886.

Married, March 13th, 1879, H. R. H. the Princess Louise Margaret Alexandra Victoria Agnes, born July 20th, 1860, daughter of H. R. H. Prince

THE ROYAL FAMILY.

Frederick Charles of Prussia, G. C. B., and has issue.

RESIDENCES: Madras; Bagshot Park, Surrey.

CLUBS: Army and Navy, Marlborough, Travelers'.

SON LIVING.

Prince Arthur Frederick Patrick Albert (Earl of Sussex), born January 13th, 1883.

DAUGHTERS LIVING.

Princess Margaret Victoria Augusta Charlotte Norah, born January 15th, 1882.

Princess Victoria Patricia Helena Elizabeth, born March 17th, 1886.

DUKE OF ALBANY.

 His Royal Highness Leopold Charles Edward George Albert, 2d Duke.

Born July 19th, 1884.

Succeeded at his birth.

SISTER LIVING.

Princess Alice Mary Victoria Augusta Pauline, born February 25th, 1883.

WIDOW LIVING OF FIRST DUKE.

Princess Helene Frederica Augusta, R. R. C.

THE ROYAL FAMILY.

(H. R. H. the Duchess of Albany), daughter of H. S. H. the Reigning Prince Waldeck and Pyrmont.

Married, April 27th, 1882, the 1st Duke, who died March 28th, 1884.

Receives an annuity of £6,000.

Residence: Claremont, Esher, Surrey.

PREDECESSOR.

[1] Princess Leopold George Duncan Albert, K. G., K. T., G. C. S. I., G. C. M. G., P. C., D. C. L., 4th son of H. M. Queen Victoria. Born April 7th, 1853.

Created Baron Arklow, Earl of Clarence, and Duke of Albany (in peerage of United Kingdom) 1881; was a Colonel in the Army and a Bencher of Lincoln's Inn.

Married, April 27th, 1882, H. S. H. the Princess Helene Frederica Augusta, daughter of H. S. H. the Reigning Prince of Waldeck and Pyrmont.

Died March 28th, 1884.

Succeeded by his son [2] Leopold Charles Edward George Albert, 2d and present Duke.

THE ROYAL FAMILY.

DUKE OF CAMBRIDGE [Her Majesty's Cousin]

Commander-in-Chief His Royal Highness George William Frederick Charles, K. G., P. C., K. P., K. T., G. C. B., G. C. H., G. M. M. G., G. C. S. I., G. C. I. E., D. C. L., LL.D., 2d Duke. Born March 26th, 1819.

Succeeded July 8th, 1850, became a Colonel in the Army 1837, Major-General 1845, Lieutenant-General 1854, General 1856, Field-Marshal 1862, and Commander-in-Chief (by Letters patent) 1887; was Colonel 17th Light Dragoons 1842–52, and of Scots Fusiliers 1852–61, and Governor of Royal Military Academy 1862-70; commanded 1st Division of Eastern Army throughout campaign of 1854, including the battles of the Alma, Balaclava, and Inkerman (horse shot) and siege of Sebastopol (medal with four clasps and Turkish medal); is Colonel-in-Chief of 17th Lancers, of R. A., of R. E., of Grenadier Guards, and of King's Royal Rifle Corps, and Honorable Colonel 3d Volunteer Batallion King's Royal Rifle Corps, and 20th (Punjab) Regiment Bengal N. I.; Pres. of Royal Military College, Sandhurst, of Royal

THE ROYAL FAMILY.

Military Academy, Woolwich, and of Christ's Hospital; Ranger of St. James, the Green, Hyde, and Richmond Parks; a Personal A. D. C. to H. M., Governor of King's College, D. C. L. of Oxford, LL.D. of Dublin, and Grand Master of Order of St. Michael and St. George, &c.; has Grand Cordon of Legion of Honor, and Grand Cross of Leopold of Belgium, &c., &c.; introduced at Privy Council 1856, and at Privy Council in Ireland 1868; receives an annuity of £12,000.

RESIDENCE: Gloucester House, Park Lane, W.

OFFICIAL RESIDENCE: Horse Guards, Whitehall, S. W.

CLUBS: Army and Navy, United Service, White's, Travelers', Junior Naval and Military, St. James', Marlborough.

SISTERS LIVING.

Princess Augusta Caroline Charlotte Elizabeth Mary Sophia Louisa (Grand Duchess of Mecklenburgh Strelitz), born July 19th, 1822; receives an annuity of £3,000.

Is a Lady of Imperial Order of Crown of India.

Married, June 28th, 1843, H. R. H. Frederick William Charles George Ernest Adolphus Gustavus, Reigning Grand Duke of Mecklenburgh Strelitz, K. G., G. C. B., and has issue.

SON LIVING.

George Adolphus Frederick Augustus Victor

THE ROYAL FAMILY.

Ernest Adalbert Gustavus William Wellington, G. C. B. (Hereditary Grand Duke), born July 22d, 1848.

Married, April 17th, 1877, the Princess Elizabeth Mary Frederica Amelia Agnes, born September 7th, 1857, daughter of H. S. H. Frederick, Reigning Duke of Anhalt; and has living issue:

Frederick George Albert Edward Ernest (Hereditary Prince), born June 17th, 1882.

Duchess Victoria Maria Augusta Louisa Antoinetta Carolina Leopoldina, born May 8th, 1878.

Duchess Augusta Charlotte Jutta Alexandra Georgiana Adolphina, born January 24th, 1880.

Residence: Mecklenburgh Strelitz.

Princess Mary Adelaide Wilhelmina Elizabeth (Duchess of Teck), born November 27th 1833.

Granted in 1866, by Act of Parliament, an annuity of £5,000.

Is a Lady of the Royal Red Cross, and of the Imperial Order of the Crown of India.

Married, June 12th, 1866, H. H. Colonel Francis Paul Charles Louis Alexander, Duke of Teck, G. C. B. The Duke of Teck was granted the title of "Highness," July 11th, 1887.

Born August 27th 1837, only son of Duke Alexander Constantine of Wurtemberg, and Claudine, Countess of Rhedey de Ris Rhedey, and of Hohenstein, Colonel (unattached), and Honorable Col-

THE ROYAL FAMILY.

onel 1st City of London Artillery Volunteers,
and of the 24th Middlesex Rifle Volunteers, and
has issue:

Sons Living: Prince Adolphus Charles Alexander Albert Edward George Philip
Louis Ladislaus, born August
13th, 1868.

Prince Francis Joseph Leopold
Frederick, born January 9th, 1870.

Is Lieutenant 8th Volunteer
Batallion Rifle Brigade (Prince
Consort's Own).

Prince Alexander Augustus
Frederick William Alfred George,
born April 14th, 1874.

Daughter Living: Princess Victoria Mary Augusta Louisa Olga Pauline
Claudine Agnes, born May
26th, 1867.

RESIDENCE: White Lodge,
Richmond Park, Surrey.

Augusta Wilhelmina Louisa (Duchess of Cambridge), daughter of H. S. H. Frederick, Land-
grave of Hesse Castle.

Born July 25th, 1797; receives an annuity of
£6,000.

Married, May 7th, 1818, H. R. H. Prince Adolphus Frederick, K. G., 1st Duke, who died July 8th, 1850, 7th son of King George III.

RESIDENCES: Ambassador's Court, St. James' Palace, S. W.; Cambridge Cottage, Kew, Surrey.

DUKE OF CUMBERLAND AND TEVIOTDALE.
[Her Majesty's Cousin.]

His Royal Highness Ernest Augustus William Adolphus George Frederick, K. G., G. C. H., 3d Duke.

Born September 21st, 1845.

Succeeded 1878.

Appointed a Colonel in British Army 1876, and a Major-General 1886; is a Colonel in Austrian Army, and Commander 42d Regiment of Infantry.

Married, December 21st, 1878, H. R. H, the Princess Thyra Amelie Caroline Charlotte Anne, C. I., born September 29th, 1853, 3d daughter of Christian IX., King of Denmark, and has issue.

RESIDENCE: Gmunden, Austria.

SONS LIVING.

Prince George William Christian Albert Ed-

THE ROYAL FAMILY.

ward Alexander Frederick Waldemar Ernest Adolph (Earl of Armagh), born October 28th 1880.

Prince Christian Frederick William George Peter Waldemar, born July 4th, 1885.

Prince—born November 17th, 1887.

DAUGHTERS LIVING.

Princess Mary Louisa Victoria Carolina Amelia Alexandra Augusta Frederica, born October 11th, 1879.

Princess Alexandra Louise Marie Olga Elizabeth Theresa Vera, born September 29th, 1882.

Princess Olga Adelaide Louise Marie Alexandra Agnes, born July 11th, 1884.

SISTERS LIVING.

Her Royal Highness the Princess Frederica Sophia Maria Henrietta Amelia Theresa, R. R. C., born 1848.

Married, April 24th, 1880, Luitbert Alexander George Lionel Alphonse, Freiherr von Pawel Rammingen, K. C. B.

RESIDENCE: Hampton Court Palace.

Her Royal Highness the Princess Mary Ernestina Josephine Adolphine Henrietta Theresa Elizabeth Alexandrina, born 1849.

These ladies only take precedence as Duke's daughters according to the date of the creation of their father's Dukedom, but as daughters of a king they are entitled to the prefix of "Royal Highness."

RESIDENCE: Gmunden, Austria.

WIDOW LIVING OF SECOND DUKE.

Her Royal Highness Alexandrina Maria Wilhelmina Catherine Charlotte Theresa Henrietta Louisa Paulina Elizabeth Frederica Georgiana [Ex-Queen of Hanover], daughter of H. S. H. Joseph, late Reigning Duke of Saxe-Altenburg.

Married, February 18th, 1843, George V.—who died 1878—King of Hanover 1851–66.

RESIDENCE: Gmunden, Austria.

PREDECESSORS.

[1] Prince Ernest Augustus, 5th son of H. M. King George III.

Created in 1799 Duke of Cumberland and Teviotdale (in peerage of Great Britain), and Earl of Armagh (in peerage of Ireland).

Succeeded to the throne of Hanover June 20th, 1837.

Died 1851.

Succeeded by his son [2] George Frederick Alexander Charles Ernest Augustus, K. G., G. C. H., 2d Duke.

Reigned as George V., King of Hanover, from November 18th, 1851 till 1866, when the Prussian Government deprived him of his throne and annexed his territory.

Was a General in the British Army.

Married, February 18th, 1843, the Princess Alexandrina Maria Wilhelmina Catherine Charlotte Theresa Henrietta Louisa Paulina Elizabeth Frederica Georgiana, daughter of H. S. H., Joseph Reigning Duke of Saxe-Altenburg.

Died June 12th, 1878.

Succeeded by his son [3] Ernest Augustus William Adolphus George Frederick, 3d and present Duke.

A CAREFULLY COMPILED
LIST OF PEERS

WHO ARE SUPPOSED TO BE EAGER TO LAY
THEIR CORONETS, AND INCIDENTALLY
THEIR HEARTS, AT THE FEET OF THE
ALL-CONQUERING AMERICAN GIRL.

———

If one should give full credit to the bitter cry
of the British-Matron-With-A-Lot-of-Marriage-
able-Daughters, he would imagine that there were
no more any eligible bachelors to be found between Land's End and John O'Groat's; that Bel-
gravia was an Adamless Eden, and Mayfair suf-
fering from a modern version of the Rape of the
Sabines, with that part of the Sabines assumed
by the British Young Man and that of the Ro-
mans by the American Girl. For the sake of international comity, however, we are glad to be
able to assure our readers that this is not so.
Diligent search by a corps of experienced explor-

ers reveals a goodly number of Britannia's sons who have not yet bowed the knee to Miss Columbia. The following catalogue of them is printed, not, of course, to hold up offers of coronets before American eyes, but to vindicate our countrywomen against the charges of wholesale spoliation. The list comprises all sorts and conditions of " eligible parties," from Dukes of prophyrogenous degree and fortunes that would make old Crœsus seem a pauper, down to the poor little heirs to Baronies of yesterday's creation whose income would make the merry iceman smile with pitying scorn. This publication will perhaps arouse the ambition of the American Girl with the prospect of other worlds to conquer; doubtless it will, as Pope prophetically wrote, " Cause hope to rise within Britannia's breast. At thought her unwed daughters may e'en yet be blest."

THE RIGHT HON. JOHN ABERCROMBIE.

Eldest son and heir of Lord Abercrombie; forty-eight years old ; educated at Harrow; formerly captain of the Rifle Brigade ; divorced from Baroness von Heidenstam of Sweden ; has no children.

The entailed estates amount to 16,000 acres, yielding an income of $75,000.

Family seats: Three Castles in Scotland.

THE HON. FREDERIC AMHERST.

Eldest son and heir of the Earl of Amherst.

The entailed estates amount to 25,600 acres, yielding an income of $200,000.

The family is very wealthy, the two previous possessors of the title having received lands, pensions, and gifts from the Crown, to the amount of over $3,000,000.

The Hon. Frederic is over fifty years old ; he served with great distinction in the navy, and subsequently as captain of the 14th Hussars.

LORD AMPTHILL

Is second Baron, twenty years of age, and was educated at Eton. He has an income of $20,0co; no landed estates. His father was the celebrated diplomatist, and belonged to the historical house of Russell. Lord Ampthill is closely related to the Duke of Bedford, Earl Russell, the Earl of Clarendon, etc.

LORD APSLEY.

Eldest son and heir of the Earl of Bathurst.

The entailed estates amount to 13,600 acres, yielding an income of $105,000.

Lord Apsley is twenty-five years old, and was educated at Eton.

Family seat : Cirencester.

THE EARL OF ANCRUM.

Eldest son and heir of the Marquis of Lothian, K. T.

The entailed estates amount to 23,000 acres, yielding an income of $260,000.

Lord Ancrum is twenty-four years of age, and a lieutenant in the army.

Family seat : Newbattle Abbey, Midlothian.

LORD ARDEE.

Eldest son and heir to the twelfth Earl of Meath.

The entailed estates amount to 15,400 acres, yielding an income of $50,000.

The Earl of Meath married an heiress, and is worth about $700,000.

Lord Ardee is in his twenty-first year.

Family seat: Kilruddery, County Wicklow, Ireland.

EARL OF ASHBURNHAM.

Is the fifth Earl, forty-nine years old; possesses entailed estates amounting to 24,500 acres, yielding an income of $125,000.

He is a Knight of Malta, and a Catholic; he has never been married.

Family seats: In Sussex and Suffolk.

THE HON. JOHN ASHBURNHAM.

Is forty-two years old, heir to the Earldom of Ashburnham; was formerly in the diplomatic service, and has a private income of about $20,000 and a country seat in Sussex.

The entailed estates amount to 24,500 acres, yielding an income of $125,000.

Family seats: Two splendid Castles in Sussex and Suffolk.

LORD ASHTOWN.

Is third Baron.

The entailed estates are at Woodlawn, County Galway, and at Kilfinane, County Limerick, Ireland. They yield but a small income, in consequence of the agricultural distress in Ireland.

Lord Ashtown is twenty-two years old, and was educated at Eton.

Family seat: Lotherton Hall, Milford Junction, Ireland.

LORD ATHLUMNEY.

Is second Baron, twenty-four years of age; was educated at Harrow, and is a lieutenant in the Coldstream Guards.

The entailed estates amount to 10,500 acres, yielding an income of $60,000.

Family seat: Somerville Castle, County Meath, Ireland.

THE EARL OF AVA.

Eldest son and heir of the first Marquis of Dufferin.

The entailed estates amount to 18,200 acres, but owing to mortgages do not yield their nominal value of $100,000 income.

Lord Ava, who is twenty-six years of age, is a lieutenant in the 17th Lancers.

Family seat: Clandeboye, County Down, Ireland.

VISCOUNT AVONMORE.

Is sixth Viscount. The entailed estates are at Roscrea, Tipperary, and at Westport, County Mayo, Ireland, and yield but a small income, owing to the agricultural distress in Ireland.

Lord Avonmore is twenty-six years of age; a lieutenant in the army.

Family seat: Belle Isle, Tipperary.

LORD BAGOT.

Is thirty-two years of age.

The entailed estates amount to 32,000 acres, yielding an income of $125,000.

He is a gentleman of the Privy Chamber.

Family seats: Blithfield Hall, Rugely, and Pool Park, Ruthin.

VISCOUNT BARING.

Is the eldest son and heir of the Earl of Northbrook.

The entailed estates amount to 10,500 acres, yielding an income of $80,000.

The Earl, who has been a Cabinet Minister and Viceroy of India, is a partner of the banking house of Baring Brothers, and inherited a personality of $8,000,000 on succeeding to the title.

Viscount Baring is thirty-six years of age ; was a captain of the Grenadier Guards and is a Member of Parliament.

Family seat : Stratton, Hampshire.

THE HON. FRANCIS BARING.

Eldest son and heir of Lord Ashburton.

The entailed estates amount to 37,000 acres, yielding an income of $250,000.

Besides having an interest in the banking house of Baring Brothers, Lord Ashburton inherited about $3,000,000 from his father.

The Hon. Francis is twenty-four years of age.

LORD BORTHWICK.

Is sixth Baron ; twenty-three years of age ; educated at Oxford.

Family seat : Ravenstone, Wigtonshire, Scotland.

LORD BENNET.

Eldest son and heir of the sixth Earl of Tankerville.

The entailed estates amount to 31,000 acres, yielding an income of $150,000.

The Earl owns the only herd of wild cattle to be found in Great Britain.

Lord Bennet, who has at present nothing but a very small allowance, has served in the navy and in the army, and is thirty-six years of age.

Family seat: Chillingham Castle, Northumberland.

LORD BERTIE.

Eldest son and heir of the eleventh Earl of Lindsay.

The entailed estates amount to 4,790 acres, yielding an income of $50,000.

Lord Bertie is twenty-seven years of age, and a lieutenant in the army.

Family seat: Uppington House, Stamford.

EARL OF BUCKINGHAMSHIRE.

Is the seventh Earl, twenty-eight years of age.

The entailed estates amount to 5,200 acres, yielding an income of $25,000.

Lord Buckinghamshire was educated at Cambridge.

LORD BOSTON.

Is sixth Baron; twenty-eight years of age; Lord-in-waiting to H. M. the Queen. He was educated at Eton and Oxford, and is a great favorite of the Queen.

The entailed estates amount to 12,500 acres, yielding an income of $77,000.

Family seats: Porthamel, Anglesey, and Hedsore Castles, near Maidenhead.

VISCOUNT BOYLE.

Is the eldest son and heir of the Earl of Shannon.

The entailed estates amount to 11,200 acres, yielding an annual income of $70,000.

The Viscount is twenty-eight years of age, was educated at Eton, and was formerly a lieutenant of the Rifle Brigade.

Family seat: Castle Martyr, Cork.

LORD BYRON.

Is ninth Baron; thirty-three years old; educated at Harrow and Oxford.

The entailed estates amount to 19,000 acres, yielding an income of $8,000.

MARQUIS DE BRISSAC.

Grandson and heir of the Duke of Brissac.

The Marquis is exceedingly wealthy, and is twenty years of age, his mother, the Vicomtesse de Tredern, being the heiress of the great French sugar refiner, Say.

Family seats : Chateau de Brissac, Anjou, and Chateau de Clermont-Gallerande, Sarthe.

THE EARL OF BURFORD.

Is the eldest son and heir of the Duke of St. Albans, who is the hereditary Lord High Falconer of England.

The entailed estates amount to 8,300 acres, yielding an income of $70,000.

The Earl is in his twentieth year, and is a godson of the Prince of Wales.

Family seat : Bestwood Lodge, Nottingham.

EARL OF CAMPERDOWN.

Is third Earl, forty-eight years old; is Lord-in-Waiting to H. M. the Queen.

Possesses entailed estates to the amount of 14,000 acres, yielding an income of $50,000.

Family seat : Camperdown, Dundee.

LORD BURGHERSH.

Is the oldest son and heir of the twelfth Earl of Westmoreland.

The entailed estates amount to 7,300 acres, yielding an income of $60,000.

The late Earl received $1,000,000 in emoluments from the Crown.

Lord Burghersh is thirty years of age, and a captain in the army.

Family seat: Apelthorpe Hall, Northamptonshire.

EARL OF CHESTERFIELD.

Is tenth Earl, thirty-three years of age.

Owns entailed estates to the amount of 13,600 acres, yielding an income of $126,000.

He was educated at Eton and Oxford, and is a barrister. He served in the army.

Family seat: Holme-Lacy, Hereford.

VISCOUNT CLIFDEN.

Is the fourth Viscount, twenty-six years old.

Possesses entailed estates to the amount of 49,-000, yielding an income of $197,000.

He was educated at Eton, and served in the army.

Family seat: Gowren Castle, Kilkenny.

LORD CARNEGIE.

Is the oldest son and heir of the ninth Earl of Southesk.

The entailed estates amount to 22,000 acres, yielding an income of $105,000.

The Earl is wealthy, having, in addition to the estates inherited, a personality of $500,000.

Lord Carnegie was educated at Harrow, is thirty-four years of age, and holds the rank of major in the army.

Family seat: Kinnaird Castle, Brechin, Scotland.

LORD CLIFFORD.

Is ninth Baron, and Count of the German Empire, a Catholic, and thirty-six years of age.

He possesses entailed estates to the amount of 8,000 acres, yielding an income of $60,000.

Among other unentailed property Lord Clifford owns an estate in the Isle of Harris worth $500,-000.

He is a barrister.

Family seat: Ugbrooke Park, Chudleigh, Devonshire.

VISCOUNT CANTELUPE.

Eldest son and heir of the seventh Earl Delawarr.

The entailed estates amount to 23,000 acres, yielding an income of $106,000.

The Earl Delawarr inherited $150,000 in cash on succeeding to the title. Viscount Cantelupe is twenty-one years of age.

Family seat: Buckhurst, Sussex.

LORD CLIFTON.

Eldest son and heir of the sixth Earl Darnley.

The entailed estates amount to 34,000 acres, yielding a rental of $190,000.

Lord Clifton is 36 years of age, was educated at Eton and Oxford, and is a distinguished zoologist. He owns Dumpton Park, Ramsgate.

Family seat: Cobham Court, Gravesend.

EARL OF CLONMEL.

Is forty-seven years of age.

Possesses entailed estates of 27,500 acres, yielding an income of $80,000.

He was formerly in the Life Guards.

Family seat: Bishopscourt, County Kildare, Ireland.

EARL OF CRAVEN.

Is fourth Earl.

The entailed estates amount to 30,700 acres, yielding a rental of $198,000.

Lord Craven, who is just twenty-one years old, has inherited a sum of $1,000,000 in ready money on attaining his majority.

County seat: Combe-Abbey, Coventry,

EARL OF DALKEITH.

Is twenty-six years of age ; eldest son and heir of the Duke of Buccleuch and Queensberry.

The entailed estates amount to 460,000 acres, yielding an income of $1,250,000.

The Duke of Buccleuch inherited $4,000,006 in cash on succeeding to the title.

VISCOUNT DRUMLANRIG.

Is the eldest son and heir of the Marquis of Queensberry. He is twenty-three years of age, in the Coldstream Guards, and very popular. He has but a small allowance, and the family is not wealthy.

Family seat: Kinmount House, County Dumfries.

VISCOUNT DEERHURST.

Is the eldest son and heir of the ninth Earl of Coventry, who is Master of Buckhounds to the Queen.

The entailed estates amount to 14,600 acres, yielding an annual income of $130,000.

Viscount Deerhurst is twenty-six years of age, and a lieutenant in the army.

Family seat: Croome Court, Worcester.

LORD DELAMERE.

Is third Baron.

The entailed estates amount to 6,700 acres, yielding an annual rental cf $59,000.

Lord Delamere is in his twentieth year.

Family seat: Vale-Royal, Northwich.

TWELFTH EARL OF DEVON.

Best known as Lord Courtenay.

The entailed estates amount to 53,000 acres, but are so heavily mortgaged that they yield nothing like the rental of $200,000, at which they are nominally valued.

Lord Devon, who is forty-eight years of age, was formerly a captain in the army and a Member of Parliament; has sown wild oats extensively.

Family seat: Powderham Castle, near Exeter.

VISCOUNT DANGAN.

Eldest son and heir of the Earl Cowley.

The entailed estates amount to 5,600 acres, yielding an annual income of $100,080.

Viscount Dangan is twenty-three years old, and a captain of militia.

Family seat: Draycot, Chippenham.

EARL OF DUDLEY.

Is the second Earl.

The entailed estates amount to 26,000 acres, yielding an income of $625,000.

The Earl, who is twenty-two years of age, inherited from his father personal property to the amount of $7,000,000.

The family jewels represent a value of $3,000,000 more.

Family seat: Witley Court, Worcester.

VISCOUNT ENNISMORE.

Eldest son and heir of the third Earl of Listowel.

The entailed estates amount to 35,500 acres, yielding an income of $100,000.

Lord Ennismore is twenty-four years of age, and a lieutenant of the Royal Scots Regiment.

Family seat: Convamore House, County Cork, Ireland.

VISCOUNT DUNGARVAN.

Is the eldest son and heir of the ninth Earl of Cork and Orrery.

The entailed estates amount to 38,300, acres, yielding a rental of $80,000.

The present Earl inherited $2,000,000 on succeeding to the title.

Viscount Dungarvan is twenty-seven years of age, and a captain of militia.

Family seat : Marston House, Frome.

VISCOUNT ENCOMBE.

Eldest son and heir of the third Earl of Eldon.

The entailed estates amount to 25,500 acres, yielding an income of $145,000.

The family is very wealthy, its founder, the famous Lord Chancellor of King George IV., having received a sum of no less than $8,000,000 from the Crown.

Viscount Encombe is in his twentieth year.

Family seat : Encombe, Wareham.

LORD ERSKINE.

Eldest son and heir of the Earl of Mar and Kellei.

The entailed estates amount to 8,000 acres, yielding an income of $28,000.

The Earl inherited a personality of $150,000, and is Premier Viscount of Scotland.

Lord Erskine is twenty-four years of age, was educated at Eton, and is a lieutenant in the army.

Family seat : Alloe House, Clackmannanshire.

VISCOUNT GAGE.

Is fifth Viscount.

The entailed estates amount to 12,330 acres, yielding an income of $70,000.

Lord Gage, who is thirty-three years of age, and who was educated at Eton and Oxford, inherited a sum of $500,000 in ready money on coming of age.

Family seat : Firle Place, Lewes.

LORD GARIOCH.

Eldest son and heir of the thirty-third Earl of Mar.

The entailed estates amount to 6,000 acres, yielding an income of $18,000.

The Earl of Mar is Premier Earl of Scotland.

Lord Garioch is twenty-two years of age, and was educated at Eton and Cambridge.

THE HON. WILLIAM GIBSON.

Eldest son and heir of Lord Ashbourne, Lord Chancellor of Ireland.

No family estates or entailed property.

Lord Ashbourne has a private income of about $40,000.

The Hon. William is twenty-one years of age, and was educated at Trinity College, Dublin.

LORD GILLFORD.

Eldest son and heir of the fourth Earl of Clanwilliam.

The entailed estates amount to 7,000 acres, yielding an income of $42,000.

The present Earl of Clanwilliam inherited a fortune of $2,000,000 from his predecessor.

Lord Gillford is twenty-one years of age, and is lieutenant in the Royal Navy.

Family seat: Gillhall, County Down, Ireland.

VISCOUNT GLENTWORTH.

Eldest son and heir of the third Earl of Limerick.

The entailed estates amount to 8,700 acres, yielding an income of $75,000.

Lord Glentworth is twenty-six years of age, and a lieutenant of the Rifle Brigade.

Family seat: Dromore Castle, County Limerick, Ireland.

LORD GREENOCK.

Eldest son and heir of the third Earl of Cathcart.

The entailed estates amount to 5,500 acres, yielding an income of $40,000.

The Countess of Cathcart is an heiress in her own right, and very rich.

Lord Greenock is thirty-two years of age, and formerly a captain in the Scots Guards.

Family seat: Thornton-le-Street, Thirsk, Yorkshire.

MARQUIS OF HAMILTON.

Eldest son and heir of the Duke of Abercorn.

Is twenty years of age.

The entailed estates amount to 78,000 acres, yielding an income of $275,000.

He is a godson of the Prince of Wales, who is a warm friend of the Duke of Abercorn.

The latter is a brother of the Marchioness of Blandford, first and divorced wife of the Duke of Marlborough.

LORD FREDERIC HAMILTON.

Is the third brother of the Duke of Abercorn. He is thirty-two years of age, was formerly in the diplomatic service, and has sat in Parliament for Manchester.

He has an allowance of $6,000 a year.

LORD HAWKE.

Is seventh Baron.

The entailed estates amount to 6,187 acres, yielding an income of $40,000.

Lord Hawke is twenty-nine years old, educated at Eton and Cambridge, and is captain of militia.

Family seat: Wighall Park, Tadcaster.

LORD JOHN HERVEY.

Is brother and heir to the Marquis of Bristol.

The entailed estates amount to 32,000 acres, yielding an income of $202,000.

Lord Hervey is forty-two years old; was major in the army.

Family seat: Tickworth Park, Bury Street, Edmunds.

EARL OF HUNTINGDON.

Is the fourteenth Earl.

The entailed estates amount to 13,600 acres, yielding an income of $35,000.

The Earl is twenty-one year of age, and a lieutenant of militia.

Family seat: Sharavogul, King's County, Ireland.

LORD ERNEST HAMILTON.

Is the fourth brother of the Duke of Abercorn;
thirty years old; formerly captain in the 11th
Hussars; Member of Parliament for North-Tyron,
and has an allowance of $6,000 a year.

LORD KENYON.

Is fourth Baron.

The entailed estates amount to 8,000 acres,
yielding an income of $60,000.

Lord Kenyon is twenty-five years of age; educated at Eton and Oxford, and is a lieutenant of
militia.

Family seat: Gredington, Shropshire.

LORD KESTEVEN.

Is second Baron.

The entailed estates amount to 6,000 acres,
yielding an income of $55,000.

Lord Kesteven, who is thirty-six years of age,
and was educated at Eton and Cambridge, inherited $150,000 in ready money on succeeding to the
title.

Family seat: Casewick Hall, Lincolnshire.

VISCOUNT KYNNAIRD.

Is the eldest son and heir of the sixth Earl of Newburgh.

The Earl is also Prince of Justiniani and Duke of Montdragone, in the Kingdom of Italy.

Lord Kynnaird is twenty-eight years of age.

The family residence is at Rome, Italy.

LORD LANGFORD.

Is fourth Baron.

The entailed estates amount to 9,700 acres, yielding an income of $40,000.

Lord Langford is thirty-eight years of age, a colonel of Grenadier Guards, and States Steward to the Viceroy of Ireland.

Family seat: Summerhill House, County Meath, Ireland.

EARL OF LEWES.

Is the eldest son and heir of the Marquis of Abergavenny.

The entailed estates amount to 28,500 acres, yielding an income of $153,000.

Lord Lewes is thirty-five years of age, and was educated at Eton.

Family seat: Eridge Castle, Tonbridge-Wells.

EARL OF LONGFORD.

Is fifth Earl.

The entailed estates amount to 20,000 acres, yielding an income of $240,000.

Lord Longford is twenty-four years of age, and a lieutenant in the Life Guards.

Family seat: Pakenham Hall, County Westmeath, Ireland.

LORD LOUGHBOROUGH.

Is the eldest son and heir of the Earl of Rosslyn.

The entailed estates amount to 3,300 acres, yielding an income of $60,000.

Lord Loughborough is in his twenty-second year.

Family seat: Dysart House, Scotland.

LORD LURGAN.

Is third Baron.

The entailed estates amount to 15,200 acres, yielding an income of $102,000.

Lord Lurgan is thirty years of age; was formerly lieutenant in the Grenadier Guards, and has been Lord-in-Waiting to the Queen.

Family seat: Brownlow Park, Lurgan, County Armagh.

VISCOUNT MAITLAND.

Is the eldest son and heir of the thirteenth Earl of Lauderdale; is twenty-one years of age, and a lieutenant of the 2d Dragoons.

Family seat: Thirlestane Castle, Scotland.

VISCOUNT MARSHAM.

Is the eldest son and heir of the fourth Earl of Romney.

The entailed estates amount to 4,900 acres, yielding an income of $65,000.

Viscount Marsham is twenty-five years of age, and a captain in the army.

Family seat: The Mote, Maidstone.

THE HON. JAMES McGAREL-HOGG.

Is the eldest son and heir of Lord Magheramorne.

The entailed estates amount to 3,500 acres, yielding an income of $20,000.

Lord Magheramorne, chairman of the late Metropolitan Board of Works, married an heiress, and is worth about $3,000,000. The Hon. James is twenty-seven years old, and a lieutenant in the Life Guards.

Family seat: Magheramorne, County Antrim, Ireland.

MARQUIS DE MacMAHON.

Is the eldest son and heir of the Marshal de MacMahon, Duke de Magenta, Knight of the Golden Fleece, and formerly President of the French Republic.

The Marquis de MacMahon is thirty-three years old, and a captain in the French Army.

Family seat: La Foresterie, near Tours.

Residence: Paris.

VISCOUNT MOLYNEUX.

Is the eldest son and heir of the fourth Earl of Sefton, K. G.

The entailed estates amount to 20,300 acres, yielding an income of $200,000.

The Earl inherited a sum of $250,000 in cash.

The Viscount is twenty-three years of age, and a lieutenant in the army.

Family seat: Crosteth Hall, Liverpool.

LORD MORETON.

Is the eldest son and heir of the third Earl of Ducie.

The entailed estates amount to 14,000 acres, yielding an annual income of $110,000.

Lord Moreton is thirty-two years of age, and has sat in Parliament.

Family seat: Tortworth Castle, Talfield.

PRINCE DE LA MOSKOWA.

Is descended from the famous Marshal Ney, is in his twentieth year, and is very wealthy, his mother being the heiress of the banker Heine.

Residences: Paris and Versailles.

THE EARL OF MULGRAVE.

The eldest son of the Marquis of Normanby, G. C. B.

The entailed estates amout to sixty-eight acres, yielding an income of $48.000.

The Earl is forty-two years old, and a clergy-man of the Church of England. He is Vicar of St. Mark's Worseley.

Family seat: Mulgrave Hall, near Whitby.

LORD NEWTOWN-BUTLER.

Eldest son of the sixth Earl of Lanesborough.

The entailed estates amount to 16,300 acres, yielding an income of $80,000.

Lord Newton-Butler is twenty-four years of age, and was educated at Eton.

Family seat: Lanesborough Lodge, County Cavan, Ireland.

LORD RICHARD NEVILL.

Is the sixth son of the Marquis of Abergavenny. twenty-six years old; educated at Eton and Cambridge, and is a private secretary to the Lord President of the Privy Council.

His present income is $7,000.

EARL OF NORBURY.

Is the fourth Earl.

The entailed estate is at Darrow Park, King's County, Ireland, but only yield a small income, owing to the agricultural distress.

The Earl is twenty-six years of age, and was educated at Harrow and Oxford.

Residence: Onslow Gardens, London.

THE HON. LYULPH OGILVY.

Is brother and heir presumptive to the Earl of Airlie.

The entailed estates amount to 70,000 acres, yielding an income of $148,000.

The Hon. Lyulph is twenty-six years of age, was formerly in the army, and is now cattle-ranching in Colorado.

Family seats: Airlie, Clune and Keltie Castles, in Scotland.

MARQUIS DU PLANTY.

Is twenty-two years of age; was formerly in the navy; possesses also the title of Marquis de Sourdy.

No less than fourteen members of the Du Planty family are recorded by Froissart's Chronicles as having fallen at the battle of Agincourt.

The family traces its descent to the time of the first Crusade.

Family seat: Chateau du Planty, Picardie, France.

LORD PORCHESTER.

Eldest son and heir of the fourth Earl of Carnarvon.

The entailed estates amount to 36,000 acres, yielding an income of $200,000.

Lord Porchester is twenty-four years of age, and was educated at Eton and Cambridge.

Family seat: Highclere Castle, Newbury.

VISCOUNT RAYNHAM.

The eldest son and heir of the fifth Marquis of Townshend.

The entailed estates amount to 19,900 acres, yielding an income of $115,000.

The Viscount is twenty-four years of age, and was educated at Oxford.

Family seat: Raynham Hall, Norfolk.

LORD RODNEY.

Is seventh Baron.

The entailed estates amount to 6,200 acres, yielding an income of $38,000.

Lord Rodney is in receipt of a hereditary pension from the Crown of $10,000.

He is thirty-two years of age, and a captain of the Life Guards Regiment. He took part in the Egyptian campaigns.

Family seat: Berrington, Leominster.

———

THE HON. LIONEL ROTHSCHILD.

Eldest son and heir of the first Lord Rothschild.

The entailed estates amount to 15,000 acres, yielding an income of $110,000.

Lord Rothschild is the chief of the banking house of that name, and inherited an English personality of $15,000,000 from his father.

The Hon. Lionel is twenty-two years of age, and an enthusiastic zoologist.

Family seat: Tring Park, Hertfordshire.

LORD ROSEHILL.

Eldest son and heir of the Earl of Northesk.

The entailed estates amount to 7,900 acres, yielding an income of $48,000.

The Earl is wealthy, having, in addition to the estates inherited, a personality of $1,000,000.

Lord Rosehill is twenty-four years of age, and a lieutenant in the army.

Family seat: Ethic Castle, Forfarshire.

VISCOUNT ROYSTON.

Eldest son and heir of the Earl of Hardwicke.

The entailed estates amount to 19,300 acres, yielding an income of $130,000.

The Earl of Hardwicke inherited a sum of $700,000 on coming into the title.

Viscount Royston is twenty-two years of age, and a lieutenant of militia.

Family seat; Wimpolt Hall, Cambridgeshire

LORD SOUTHAMPTON.

Is fourth Baron.

The entailed estates amount to 6,800 acres, yielding an income of $45,000.

Lord Southampton is twenty-three years of age, and is a lieutenant of the 10th Hussars.

Family seat: Aynhoe Park, Banbury.

THE EARL OF SANDWITH.

Is the eighth Earl.

The entailed estates amount to 11,300 acres, yielding an income of $80,000.

Besides the estates, the Earl inherited a personality of $2,000,000.

He is forty-five years of age, and a colonel in the army.

Family seat: Hinchinghoke, Huntingdon.

THE EARL OF SCARBOROUGH.

Is the tenth Earl.

The entailed estates amount to 21,600 acres, yielding an income of $160,000.

Besides the estates, the Earl has inherited a personality of $500,000.

He is thirty-two years of age, and a captain of the 7th Hussars.

Family seat: Lumley Castle, Durham.

VISCOUNT ST. CYRES.

Eldest son and heir of the second Earl of Iddesleigh.

The entailed estates amount to 5,600 acres, yielding an income of $30,000.

Lord St. Cyres is in his twenty-first year.

Family seat: Pines, Exeter.

LORD SKELMERSDALE.

Eldest son and heir of the first Earl of Lathom, Lord Chamberlain to the Queen.

The entailed estates amount to 7,200 acres, and yield an income of $107,000.

Lord Skelmersdale is twenty-four years old, and is a lieutenant in the Horse Guards.

Family seat: Lathom Hall, Lancashire.

VISCOUNT SOMERTON.

The eldest son and heir of the third Earl of Normanton.

The estates are all in Ireland, and their value has suffered considerably by the decrease of rents in that country.

The Viscount is thirty-one years of age, served in the 7th Hussars, and owns in his own right the estate of Woodgate's Park, near Salisbury.

Family seat: Somerley, Ringwood, Hampshire.

THE EARL OF STRADBROKE.
Is third Earl.

The entailed estates amount to 12,203 acres, yielding an income of $77,000.

In addition to the estates, the Earl inherited a personality of $900,000.

He is twenty-eight years of age, and holds the rank of major in the army.

Family seat: Henham Hall, Suffolk.

VISCOUNT SUDLEY.

Eldest son and heir of the Earl of Arran.

The entailed estates amount to 44,000 acres, yielding an income of $55,000.

The family has received about $2,500,000 from the Crown during the past century.

Viscount Sudley is twenty-one years of age, and is lieutenant in the army.

Family seat: Castle Gore, County Mayo, Ireland.

PRINCE HELY DE TALLEYRAND-PERIGORD.

Eldest son of the Prince de Sagan, and grandson of the Duke of Talleyrand, who is also Duke of Valencey and Duke of Sagan.

Prince Hely is twenty-eight years of age, and enormously wealthy.

In addition to the immense entailed estates of the family, he will inherit his mother's great fortune. He visited New York last year.

Residence: Rue St. Dominique, Paris.

PRINCE DE TARENTE.

Eldest son and heir of the Duke de la Tremoille.

The Prince is twenty-six years of age.

The family is very wealthy and very ancient.
Residence: Paris.

LORD TENTERDEN.

Is fourth Baron.

There are no entailed estates, and Lord Tenterden's income is barely over $6,000, but his stepmother is wealthy.

He is twenty-four years of age, and a lieutenant in the army.

Residence: 17 Portland Place, London.

LORD TEWKESBURY.

Eldest son and heir of the Earl of Munster.

There are no entailed estates, and the family is very poor.

The grandfather of Lord Tewkesbury was an illegitimate son of King William IV.

Lord Tewkesbury is thirty years of age, and a captain in the army.

Residence: Palmeira Square, Brighton.

VISCOUNT THROWLEY.

Eldest son and heir of the Earl of Sondes.

The entailed estates amount to 19,000 acres, producing an annual income of $150,000.

The earl is quite wealthy, having in addition to the estates inherited a personality of $400,000.

The Viscount is twenty-eight years of age, and a captain in the army.

Family seat: Leas Court, Faversham.

VISCOUNT VELLETORT.

Eldest son and heir of the fourth Earl of Mount-Edgcumbe.

The entailed estates amount to 18,200, acres, yielding an income of $124,000.

The Marquis is Lord High Steward of H. M. the Queen.

Viscount Velletort is twenty-four years old, and a lieutenant in the army.

The family is very wealthy.

Family seat: Mount-Edgcumbe, Davenport.

EARL OF WESTMEATH.

Is eleventh Earl

Possesses the estates of Pallas, County Galway, and Eastwell, near Kilrickle.

The Earl is in his twentieth year.

Family seat: Pallas, County Galway.

THE HON. HARRY TYRWHITT-WILSON.

Eldest son and heir of Sir Henry Tyrwhitt-Wilson, Bart., and of the Baroness Birners, to whose Barony he will succeed.

He is thirty-two years of age, was formerly in the Grenadier Guards, and is equerry to the Prince of Wales.

He personally owns Keythorpe Hall, Leicester, and has a yearly allowance of about $20,000.

VISCOUNT GREY-DE-WILTON.

Is the eldest son of the fourth Earl of Wilton.

The entailed estates amount to 9,800 acres, yielding an income of $152,000.

Besides the estates, the present Earl of Wilton has inherited a personality of $600,000.

The Viscount is twenty-six years of age.

Family seat: Heaton Park, W. Manchester.

———

THE MARQUIS OF WINCHESTER.

Is the fifteenth Marquis and Premier Marquis in the Peerage of Great Britain. He is also the Hereditary Bearer of the Cap of Maintenance.

The entailed estates amount to 4,700 acres, yielding an income of $22,000.

He is thirty-two years of age, and a captain of the Coldstream Guards.

Family seat: Amport House, Hampshire.

———

LORD WOLVERTON.

Is third Baron.

There are no entailed estates, but Lord Wolverton has a personal income of $75,000.

He is twenty-eight years old, somewhat delicate, and was educated at Harrow.

Residence: 32 Eaton Place, London.

MARQUIS OF WORCESTER.

Eldest son and heir of the eight Duke of Beaufort.

The entailed estates amount to 52,000 acres, yielding an income of $260,000.

The Marquis of Worcester is forty years of age, and was formerly a captain in the Horse Guards.

The Duke of Beaufort is entitled to quarter the Royal Arms of England, being descended from John of Gaunt.

Family seats: Badminton, Stroke-Gifford, and Llanganock Park.

DUKE OF UZES.

Is in his twentieth year, exceedingly wealthy, and holds the title of Premier Duke of France.

The Duke owns the whole of the town of Uzes in the valley of the Rhone. His mother is the heiress of the celebrated Veuve Cliquot, of champagne fame.

Family seat: Chateau d'Uzes, Uzes, Rhone.

THE GREAT BALL OF 1890.

The greatest assemblage of social notabilities, representing the wealth and fashion of the chief city of the Union, and comprising celebrities from all parts of the country, took place on the evening of January 2, 1890, at the Metropolitan Opera House.

In it were gathered the representatives of New York's best society, the recognized leaders of the charming circle wherein youth, beauty, culture, refinement, meet to exchange confidences and compliments.

At this grand ball there were nearly eleven hundred person, and it was certainly, considering the social standing of those present, the most notable event of the age. The arrangements were under the control of Mr. Ward McAllister, and the elaborate programme, with its numerous details, was carried out with an accuracy of movement that knew no jar or hitch, and reflected the greatest credit on the energetic and courteous gentleman who planned it.

The entrance to the Opera House was made through the big swinging doors of the edifice, the glasses of which had been partly obscured by silken hangings. After passing a second series of doors, a scene such as has rarely met even the most traveled burst upon the eye. With it came the intoxicating odor of countless flowers, made more sweet by the spicy exhalation of the winter foliaged forest trees that were partly seen and partly obscured everywhere.

All the familiar accessories of the place were hidden. There was to be seen nothing but a dense mass of green, and of that shade of green, too, which one encounters only in the forests of Georgia and Florida. The walls were of clinging Southern vines, so thickly interwoven that through no space showed the old rose of the original surface. Against this almost black-green background stood palm trees, their long spear-like leaves waving, as one by one the guests arrived and brought with them a draught from the night. The ceiling, with its warm coloring, was left untouched, but the vines were so profuse and so natural in their training that instead of a flat top to this avenue leading to the many attractive scenes yet to come, angles were all removed and a dome of verdure was formed.

Separating the lobby from the foyer were three arches, reinforced by a graceful series of iron gates. The scheme of decoration was carried to these, which were nothing more than great columns of trailing clematis, with the beautiful

Southern moss clinging here and there, just as though one had entered the Everglades and had found a doubly enchanted spot. The clematis climbed everywhere, clung everywhere. It trailed over the iron gates until they became nothing more nor less than screens of verdure, whose waxy leaves reflected the soft light which was thrown upon them by the clusters of incandescent electric lights, which, like the grapes of the Promised Land, hung in great clusters, and shed their radiance on either side of this screen, which was to part from the elect of society those whose business it was merely to attend upon their employers. These lights were suspended from the center of each arch, and as there were one hundred of them in this comparatively confined space, the brilliancy of the entrance may be appreciated.

Passing between these verdure-clad gates, the fortunate attendants found themselves in what was a most charmingly reproduced tropical garden. The trailing vines and clinging moss became more luxuriant. There was no break in the masses of green here, for, as the boxes were not used, the broad stair-ways flanking the main entrance were transformed into terraces whereon, with a foundation of mosses and ivy, stood palm trees, rising each row a little loftier than the other, the light green of the palm intermingling with the darker green of the orange trees, whose golden fruit sent forth new and still sweeter odors to meet each new-comer. The way leading to the supper rooms was formed of an arch of foliage. The balcony which overhangs the main entrance was backed and surmounted with orange and palm trees, while from the ceiling hung the clematis and the Southern moss, whose gracefully waving fibers made the upper portion of this bit of decoration seem to be instinct with the animation of some breezy Georgian woodland. Overhanging the balcony were more clematis and ivy, forming an unbroken green background.

The sides of the stairways were covered with verdure, and it was surrounded by this wealth of springtime in the midst of winter that one passed beneath this legend of celebration as well as of welcome, and passed into the dimly-lighted yet beautiful grotto, which was the preliminary halting point before the ball-room was reached.

Beneath the balcony the ceiling at the joining of the two corridors which encircle the big auditorium was covered with clematis, with great masses of moss, and with stray garlands of smilax. On either side stood palm and orange trees, the latter bearing fruit. The branches of the leaves and hanging vines formed an apparently almost impenetrable grotto, the shadows in which the light which came dimly from the clusters within the arches served to increase rather than dispel. In order that the illusion should not be broken, and that the imaginative might easily believe themselves actually within a forest glade, the continuation of the corridors, where were situated the hat and cloak rooms, was screened by a big cypress tree at each angle. Thus the continuity of the foliage was unbroken even when the folding doors, which permitted entrance to the auditorium of the Opera House, were encountered. These, too, were clad in green, curtains of English ivy hanging over them, but not in such a way as to interfere with their very necessary working. The little passageway leading upward to the dancing floor was screened, so far as its walls were concerned, with clematis. It was when issuing from this that the full beauty of the house, which had been so exquisitely decorated by Klunder, was peceived.

IN THE BALL-ROOM.

The first thing which impressed one was that there were no boxes. If there was tropical luxuriance without, here was Northern springtime freshness and color, and the fairest blossoms that bloom in the early year. The great extent of the auditorium would have made any less lavish decoration seem meager, indeed. The scheme of the decorator was to give those persons who were near the proscenium arch an idea of the immensity of the ball-room by making the great masses of foliage take a gradual progression toward the center and top of the house, so that looking in the direction of the entrance it was as though one were gazing upon the side of a precipitous mountain with all its manifold verdure and wealth of flowers. The illusion, even in the brilliancy bestowed upon the room by twelve hundred electric lights, was nearly perfect. The one exclamation heard from all who entered that beautiful room was " How lovely," or " This is a veritable forest!" The decorator had taken Turkey red and had festooned the fronts of all the boxes and the galleries with it. This deprived the house of its usually cold effects on account of its undecided decorations, and gave as a basis for all the superimposed verdure and flowers a warmth of background which added infinitely to the value of their own beauties.

The first tier of boxes was effectively concealed by trees in full foliage, lifting their heads fully forty feet. They were representations of the winter forest beauty of the North, South, and West, and they gave a foundation to the masses of color and verdure which extended nearly three times the distance to the dome. In these trees were hung great clusters of daffodils and tulips, the yellow of the one and the scarlet of the others mak-

ing bits of gorgeous coloring in the shades cast
by the tree boughs. Above the rail of the first
tier of boxes just peeped the tops of tiny holly,
laurel, and cypress trees. These were backed by
still taller ones, so that the interiors of the stalls,
which played so important a part during the opera
season, were completely filled. But the dark
green was not to be unrelieved, for in each box
there was a great bank of flowers. In one there
were tender and odorous white hyacinths, in another, crimson tulips nodded their heads, in a
third the yellow daffodils were as masses of gold,
while in others the white jonquils and the pale
yellow primroses rivaled each other in beauty.
The splendor resulting from this arrangement
was accentuated by the grouping of incandescent
electric lights in clusters of three, each point of
brilliancy making a queer but beautiful trefoil
glow upon the masses of flowers. This festooning of electric lights was carried entirely
around the first tier. The wealth of verdure
was made greater by the trailing of moss and
clematis over the box rail.

The second tier of boxes, still with the red
festoonings and the luxuriance of creeping vines,
had, as its chief adornment, holly, laurel, and
cypress trees of irregular height, the contrasts
of height being sustained completely around the
circle. Here again the effect of a mountain side

was simulated, and was particularly illusive. The third tier bore a mass of vines and mosses, creeping or trailing over the scarlet of the festooning. The interiors were concealed effectively by the long sprays which swung from the balcony to the family circle, whose decorations were composed of winter-green and mistletoe, their red and white berries, while not perceptible from the dancing floor, giving a feathery effect to the dense masses of green.

But all this formed only the walls of this marvelously beautiful ball-room. The ceiling was perhaps the greatest source of wonder and delight, for it carried out the idea that the dancing was done in the midst of Southern forest lands, and that the light which streamed through from above was actually the sunlight striving to find a pathway through the interlacing boughs and vines; for the ceiling of the room was made of great festoonings of clematis and ivy, with bunches of moss trailing their ends away below. Long streamers of clematis waved twenty-five feet below the auditorium, while irregularly placed in this verdant luxuriance were one hundred stars, each six feet in diameter, covered with the filmiest blue and white paper. They either swung in the air or rested upon the vines, and through all of this streamed the light from the great central chandelier of the Opera House, many feet above. This filtered light, together with the electric lights, along the first tier, and another row making the third tier brilliant, furnished the entire illumination of the dancing floor, but it was exceedingly mellow, and consequently charming.

The separation by means of the proscenium arch of the main auditorium from the stage was not permitted to be in any sense conspicuous. The vines which made the box and gallery fronts so beautiful, were trained around the sides of the arch, entirely concealing it, and making of the stage an enormous alcove. The result warranted sacrificing this, for the integrity of the ball-room was sustained. The scenery on the stage was a landscape, and in it reminiscences of Siegfried and the Rhine maidens. To make it more realistic were countless palm trees and exotics, while upon a terrace which extended about the sides of the stage were lilies, azaleas, and roses, all blooming in the soil in which their seeds burst. Beneath the boughs of the trees seats were placed, and there, throughout the night, were the gayest of all the gay scenes enacted, for not alone was this the flower garden of this forest-like dancing pavilion, but from it could be secured the most complete view of all the splendors of the decorations. There were hundreds of electric lights here, too, and their brilliancy seemed heightened by the richer colors of summer flowers which were set apart in it.

OPENING THE BALL.

Once within the ball-room, surrounded by this extraordinary profusion of verdure and flowers, one only became aware of the reality of the merrymaking a la mode by his name being announced by a footman, arrayed in scarlet plush, who stood at the corner of the entrance. Servants, clothed in plush and in private livery had been everywhere without, at the great floral screen in the lobby, in the foyer, at set spaces of ten feet in the corridor, at the gentlemen's coat-rooms in the Fortieth street vestibule; serving maids had been in the ladies' salons on the parterre corridor, and ten more had been ready to dispose of the ladies' cloaks in racks which had been built for them on either side of the same corridor; but in this profusion of floral decoration one had no chance to appreciate how perfectly had been arranged every detail of service and protection.

Though few of the guests of the committee had arrived before eleven o'clock, yet when that hour struck on a set of silver chimes in one of the corridors, the New Year's ball was officially open.

There were three of the most admired ladies in the society of the city ready to receive, and as one's name was announced he was welcomed by

Mrs. William Astor, Mrs. De Lancey Kane, and Mrs. Elliott Roosevelt. Mrs. Astor wore a Worth gown of extraordinary beauty. It was of a light brocade, with a very long train of the same material. The bodice was decollete. She wore a stomacher of diamonds, a diamond tiara, and her famous necklace of brilliants. She was perhaps the most noticeable of the group. Mrs. Kane's costume was an elaborate one of white brocade, also with a long train and low-cut bodice. She, too, wore some beautiful jewels and flowers. Mrs. Roosevelt's gown was of white silk, covered with white tulle. The left side of the skirt had a panel of cloth of gold, and the bodice was also of cloth of gold, made decollete, edged about the shoulders with white feathers. The garniture was of white flowers. She, too, wore many diamonds.

They stood not more than ten feet from the entrance to the dancing floor. As the guests passed them they were met by the gay strains of Strauss' "Vienna Women," played by the Hungarian orchestra, and they were soon whirling over the big plane in a waltz. Though the ball was an early one, the auditorium of the Opera House did not appear to be well filled with the dancers until quite 11:30 o'clock. Then, however, the corridors and the entrance vestibule were filled with a superbly dressed and chattering crowd, all expressing gratification at the surroundings, and all anxious to get within.

Almost by the time the second number of the dancing list had been concluded, there were visits made to the corridors on the Fortieth street side, where Pinard had laid a beautifully decorated buffet, on which were found lemonade, champagne punch, bouillon, tea, and coffee. The abundance of the provision was so plentiful that many who appeared here to remedy the fatigues of the first dance or two, and were informed that the supper rooms were open, returned to the dancing floor to wait until after the *quadrille d'honneur* had become a thing of the past. But those who remained regretted their impatience because of the deprivation of enjoyment of the things to come in the assembly rooms above.

When the first two dances were ended the ball may have been described as a success, for there was present that element of enjoyment which most great balls lack, the sense of security that one's neighbor in the dance might well be one's personal guest. This pleasurable sociability, without which any assembly is a failure, was evident from the outset. Every one either knew every one else or, wanted to. In quick succession came this dance music, every number filling the great dancing floor to a larger proportion :

THE GREAT BALL.

Polka, " La Visite.".................Lander.
Waltz, " Tout Paris.".............Waldteufel.
Polka, " Electra.".............Frankenstein
Lancers, " Clover."....................Suppe.

It was promptly at one o'clock when, from the musicians' inclosure, came a fanfare of cornets, clear and ringing, bringing the loiterers in the supper-rooms and the corridors hurrying to the great apartment within.

All knew that the chief event of the evening was to take place. The ninty-six chosen, whose presence in the *quadrille d'honneur* was because of their indisputable right to claim the respect of their fellows, were to go through the stately measures of Sir Roger de Coverley. It is true that the movement was that of a Virginia reel, but it was the reel of the early part of the century —not the rollicking, dashaway romp which it is sometimes made now. It became a slow and graceful movement, whose advances, pauses, salutes, and courtesies were as stately as the music and as dignified as the participants in the dance.

Persons who had the good fortune to witness this ceremonious minuet will not soon forget it. Surrounded by the most beautiful environment, the four sets, each with twelve ladies and twelve gentlemen, stretched in parallel lines across the width of the room. Thus the dancing floor, with the exception of the space beyond the proscenium arch, was the moving, winding, changing, bowing succession of figures, among which were most of the beautiful women and many of the gallant men of the Nation's society. Irrespective of the grace of the dance, which proceeded to the strains of the Hungarian Band, the scene, as a spectacle, was a most brilliant one. The most magnificent costumes were blended. There was an almost dazzling effect from the splendid jewels which were worn, and which were peculiarly iridescent under the soft yet penetrating glow of the electric lights. The flowers which the ladies bore gave an additional variety of color to the mass, and the frequent glitter of some order or uniform worn by some member of the diplomatic corps gave among the men points of contrast which were as brilliant as they were charming.

The formation of the sets was calculated to give something more than ordinary ceremonial to the *quadrille d'honneur.* The debutantes were assigned to the first set, and here was a veritable garland of buds. It was a distinction of no small significance to make one's first bow to society at the New Year's ball, and so the prizes, but twenty-four in all, were eagerly disputed. The costumes were of peculiar beauty, the great use of tulle in gowns giving them a lightness which made them especially charming. The arrangement of the four sets was based upon a somewhat poetical idea of Mr. McAllister. He was desirous that social prominence should be hemmed in by beauty; that weight of dignity, that a combination of millions and ancestry, should dance with flankings of the prettiest women that New York could muster. With this end in view the two center sets of the quadrille were made up in this wise:

Mr. Ward McAllister and Mrs. Robert Goelet, Mr. Lynch Pringle, late Consul-General of the United States to Constantinople, with Mrs. Cornelius Vanderbilt; Mr. W. Bayard Cutting and Mrs. Coleman Drayton; M. le Ghent, Belgian Minister to Washington, and Mrs. Arthur Paget; Mr. Cornelius Vanderbilt and Mrs. William C. Whitney, Mr. Chauncey M. Depew and Mrs. Elliott Roosevelt, Mr. C. Francis Winthrop and Mrs. De Lancey Kane, Mr. Frederick D. Thompson and Mrs. Henry Clews, Mr. H. G. Edwardes, Secretary of the British Legation at Washington, and Mrs. Edward Cooper; Mr. William C. Whitney and Mrs. Burke-Roche, Mr. Perry Belmont and Mrs. Bradley Martin, Sir Roderick Cameron and Mrs. Paran Stevens, Mr. Lispenard Stewart and Miss Hope Goddard of Providence, R. I; Mr. John Jacob Astor, Jr., and Miss Amy Bend, Mr. Bradley Martin and Mrs. Luther Kountze, Mr. Edward Everett and Miss McAllister, Mr. J. J. Wysong and Mrs. Edward

Livingston, Mr. E. Livingston Ludlow and Mrs. J. T. Parish, Baron Halkett and Miss Sarah Phelps Stokes, Mr. A. C. Gurnee and Mrs. George B. De Forest, Mr. R. G. Hone and Mrs. Clement Moore, Mr. Robert L. Cutting and Mrs. Samuel Colgate, Mr. J. Bowers Lee and Mrs. W. D. Sloane, Mr. J. W. Beekman and Mrs. Frederick J. De Peyster.

To the left of these was a set made up of Mr. Thomas H. Howard and Mrs. August Belmont, Jr., with eleven other couples composed of the younger society people, and to the right of the two main sets was one headed by Mr. George H. Bend and Mrs. James A. Burden.

Though the measure was slow, it did not take long to complete the Sir Roger De Coverley. It was like most good things; no sooner was it begun than it was half over. In a little less than fifteen minutes, when the last strains of the band had begun to echo, the sets were breaking up, all their members with faces flushed by the gentle but exhilarating exercise, all regretting that it had not lasted just a little while longer. It was then quite 1:15 o'clock, and as at that hour the committee, composed of Mr. Cornelius Vanderbilt, Mr. Ward McAllister, and Mr. Byam K. Stevens, were to take supper, there was a general movement toward the supper-rooms, the Hungarian Band playing a march.

THE SUPPER-ROOMS.

These were reached by means of the thirty-ninth street stair-way, and partly by the Fortieth street one. As the supper-room was opened at eleven o'clock, and would remain at the service of the guests until after the cotilion was danced and the ball ended, there was not even at this time a crowd either on the stair-way or in the rooms. These apartments were the ones· known as the assembly rooms, on the parterre floor of the opera house. Pinard used all the space he had, and there was plenty of it. There were covers laid for twelve hundred persons on the two hundred small tables which occupied the apartments known as the ball-room, the concert room, the foyer, and the greenroom. There were elaborately decorated buffet tables at the sides of the ball-room and concert room, whose tops and covers, where not laden with viands, showed palms, holly, and roses. Upon them, too, stood great silver candelabra in which burned pink candles. The small tables were separated by only one main division— a broad aisle through which the guests made their way, and from which they were served Each table held, besides the service requisite for the supper, a handsomely decorated pot of palms, a bottle of champagne, and a bottle of apollinaris. Save by the plants and flowers which have been mentioned, the supper-rooms were not decorated, but there was no occasion for extra adornment, the rich mural ornaments being brought into full relief by the electric lights.

It was proved that the judgment of the committee in serving the supper in European fashion, avoiding all the delays, crowds, and thousand annoyances of a supper procession, was excellent. The continuous service, like the continuous dancing, gave every one ample time to reach that condition of contentment which comes of abundance. Even during the *quadrille d'honneur* there was very effective dancing beyond the proscenium arch by ladies and gentlemen whose names were not included in the list which the committee had been so many days arranging.

The menu of the supper was notable because of the variety, delicacy, and rarity of the food which was provided. It was printed in blue ink upon heavy bristol board, the beveled edges being gilded.

At the center-table, the one set apart for the committeemen and the lady patronesses, the order was like this: At the head sat Mr. McAllister, with Mrs. William Astor on his right; at his left was Mrs. Grover Cleveland. Then came in this order Mr. Cornelius Vanderbilt and Mrs. Elliott

Roosevelt, Byam K. Stevens and Mrs. De Lancey Kane, Count von Arco Valley, the German Minister to the United States, and Mrs. Arthur Paget; Mr. C. Francis Winthrop, Frederick D. Thompson and Mrs. Cornelius Vanderbilt, ex-President Grover Cleveland and Mrs. W. C. Whitney, Secretary of the Navy Tracy and Mrs. James P. Kernochan, Mr. Lispenard Stewart and Mrs. Bradley Martin, and Mr. J. Pierpont Morgan and Mrs. Wilmerding, daughter of Secretary Tracy. The three tables immediately adjoining this one were presided over by Mr. Lynch Pringle and Mrs. Brockholst Cutting, Mr. William C. Whitney and Mrs. J. T. Burden, and Mr. J. W. Beekman and Mrs. Frederick J. De Peyster.

It was at supper that the more prominent strangers were recognized, among them being Miss Pauncefote, daughter of the British Minister; Mrs. Edward Willing of Philadelphia, Mr. W. Biddle of Philadelphia, Mr. Nathaniel Thayer of Boston, Mr. Robert Lenox Banks of Albany, Gen. Banks, A. von Mumm, Secretary of the German Legation at Washington; J. A. W. Grip, the Swedish Minister; Mr. J. C. R. Peabody of Boston, Baron de la Grande, Gen. Van Vliet, United States Army; Mr. and Mrs. J. G. Johnson of Philadelphia, Mr. and Mrs. Amory Lawrence, Owen Whistler of Philadelphia, the Hon. Mr. and Mrs. Herbert of Washington, Senator Butler of South Carolina, and Colonel Gourauld of London.

It was while the guests were in the supper-room that the peculiar richness of the costuming was apparent. On the dancing floor there had been too much motion to make individual toilets noticeable. The groupings had been beautiful in the extreme, but the personality of the guest, and the detail of her costume, were not emphasized. It was when discussing the bountiful supply of dainties which Pinard had supplied that the astonishingly elaborate decoration of the dresses, with gold and silver embroidery, was evident. There were scarcely a score of gowns of the nearly six hundred costumes worn which did not show in some particular the embroiderer's art. The effect seemed to be, however, not so much to secure really artistic handiwork as it was to achieve effect.

There were a large number of white gowns, too; in fact, they were in a considerable majority, the material being usually of the heaviest brocades, softened by trimmings of mousseline de soie. The debutantes and the younger society women seemed to prefer tulle to almost any other of the materials, and as a result the magnificence of the dowagers was softened very pleasingly by their gauzily draped companions. The costumes also demonstrated that women with beautiful arms and necks have discovered that nothing sets them off quite so well as costumes of black, with pearl or diamond ornaments, so that the presence of these somewhat somber gowns had their decorative reasons.

While the committee was dining there was a succession of dances down stairs. It was the intention of the committee to give the young folks every chance to amuse themselves in this fashion before the time for the formal cotillon. There was much curiosity concerning the dancing of this, because it was the second time in this country in which the English custom of having a long and continuous dance would be followed, and the first time when it would be attempted on a grand scale.

There was certainly little miscalculation on the part of Mr. McAllister and his fellow-committemen when they declared that the cotillon should begin at two o'clock. By this hour, because of the preceding dances, the admirable supper, the crowning effect of the ball's unqualified success, the young people were all expectant.

At exactly 2:10 o'clock the cotillon was begun by Lander playing the waltz, Ange d'Amour," by Waldteufel, to begin. This was followed by "Maid Marion," by Reece, and "Confidences," by Waldteufel, and as polka music "Hungarian," by Lander, "Bouquet," by Dietrich," and "Puppenfee," by Bayer. There were one hundred and forty-eight couples in the cotillon, making the largest one ever danced in this country. At the signal it was led by Mr. Lispenard Stewart and Mrs. Coleman Drayton, at whose right were Mr. McAllister and Mrs. Cornelius Vanderbilt. When the last notes of " Puppenfee " had died away the New Year's ball was a thing of the past.

WHO WERE THERE.

Among the persons who were at the ball, and whose names have not been already mentioned, were the following:

A.

Mr. and Mrs. Auchmuty, Henry O. Avery, Mr. and Mrs. Francis B. Austin, William Austin, David Austin, Mr. and Mrs. Joseph S. Auerbach, Miss Alice P. Auerbach, Mr. and Mrs. John W. Auchincloss, Hugh D. Auchincloss, Mr. and Mrs. John Turner Atterbury, Mr. and Mrs. Charles L. Atterbury, Hoffman Atkinson, Mrs. Joshua Atkins, Mr. and Mrs. Thomas B. Atkins, Miss Eliza Aspinwall, J. Lawrence Aspinwall, William C. Ashwell, Mr. and Mrs. Charles Beckwith Ashmore, Mr. and Mrs. Herbert Ashmore, Mr. and Mrs. Clarence D. Ashley, Mr. and Mrs. D. S. Appleton, Mr. and Mrs. William W. Appleton, Mrs. George S. Appleton, Benjamin Arnold, Mr. and

Mrs. D. Maitland Armstrong, Mr. and Mrs. Francis B. Arnold, Mrs. and Mrs. H. O. Armour, Mrs. William H. Anthon, Mr. and Mrs. J. L. Anthony, Robert Appleton, Charles Adams Appleton, Mrs. d'Anglemont, Mr. and Mrs. William S. Andrews, Walter Scott Andrews, Mr. and Mrs. Constant A. Andrews, Mr. and Mrs. Oswald Anderson, Mr. and Mrs. James Andariese, Henry Amy, Edward C. Anderson, Mr. and Mrs. William Armory, Mrs. Henry V. Allien and the Misses Allien, Mr. and Mrs. James R. Amidon, Mr. and Mrs. Gustav Amsinck of Summit, N. J., Mr. and Mrs. Rudolph Allen, Mr. and Mrs. Alphonse H. Alger, Bryce Allen, Vanderbilt Allen, Frederick H. Allen, H. Montague Allen, Mr. and Mrs. Henry A. Alexander, Maitland Alexander, Philip Henry Adee, John G. Agar, Mr. and Mrs. Alexander McLean Agnew, Mrs. Cornelius Agnew, the Misses Agnew, Mr. and Mrs. Joseph Agostini, Mr. and Mrs. Percy Alden, Mr. and Mrs. Spencer Aldrich, John H. Allen, Miss Daisy Allen.

B.

Mr. and Mrs. August Belmont, Mr. N. Beckwith, Miss Beckwith, Mr. and Mrs. C. Berryman, Mr. and Mrs. Lloyd Bryce, Livingston Beekman, Miss Amy Bend, Mr. and Mrs. Harry Babcock, Samuel Babcock, the Misses Babcock, Charles Backman, Mr. and Mrs. Lathrop Bacon, Mr. and

Mrs. George Butterworth, Mr. and Mrs. Joseph Busk, I. Adriance Bush, Mr. and Mrs. Arthur Burtis, David Wolfe Bruce, Mr. and Mrs. John Scott Browning, Mr. and Mrs. Frederick Brown, Miss Brooker, Mr. and Mrs. Arthur Page Brown, Mr. and Mrs. H. L. Brevoort, Mr. and Mrs. Otterbourne Bright, Mr. and Mrs. George Bradish and Miss Amy Bradish, Mr. and Mrs. John Boynton, Miss Boynton, Mr. and Mrs. Lawrence Breese and Miss Heloise Breese, Mr. and Mrs. George Bowdoin and Miss Bowdoin, Mr. and Mrs. Samuel Borrowe and the Misses Borrowe, Edgar Hatfield Booth, Mr. and Mrs. Matthew Borden, John Boardman and the Misses Boardman, Carrington Bolton, George Bliss, Mr. and Mrs. George Blanchard, Mr. and Mrs. Birdseye Blakeman, Mr. and Mrs. David Bishop, Mr. and Mrs. George Betts, the Misses Betts, Mr. and Mrs. E. R. Biddle, Mr. and Mrs. Fred Billings and the Misses Billings, W. H. Bingham, Mrs. Annie Bettner, Mr. and Mrs. Gionori Bettini, Mr. and Mrs. Benkard, Henry Bennett, E. P. K. Benson, Arthur Benjamin, Gerard Beekman and Miss Beekman, Mr. and Mrs. Carroll Beckwith, Mrs. Henry Baxter, Andrew Bibby.

C.

Mrs. Chapman, Mr. and Mrs. Clarkson, Miss Clarkson, Mr. and Mrs. H. A. Coster, Miss Martha Coster, Mr. and Mrs. C. Coster, Miss Adeline

Coster, Mrs. Hayward Cutting, Mrs. George Curtis, Miss Constance Curtis, Mr. and Mrs. W. Wetmore Cryder, Miss Cryder, Mrs. B. E. Cruger, Mr. and Mrs. Walter Crosby, R. Fleming Crooks, David Crocker, Mrs. George Crocker, David Crawford, Miss Crawford, Mr. and Mrs. David William N. Crane, Miss Crane, Mr. and Mrs. Samuel D. Craig, Mr. and Mrs. H. B. Coxe, Mr. and Mrs. Jennings S. Cox and Miss Cox, Mr. and Mrs. Frederic R. Coudert, the Misses Coudert, Mrs. Charles Coster, Miss Coster, Mr. and Mrs. Birdsall Cornell, Mr. and Mrs. George Coppell, the Misses Coppell, Mr. and Mrs. Charles A. Coombs, William Coombs, Mr. and Mrs. Henry H. Cook, Miss Cook, Mr. and Mrs. Frederick A. Constable, Frederick Conkling, Miss Laura Conkling, Mr. and Mrs. Harris Colt, Mr. and Mrs. Clarence R. Conger, Mr. and Mrs. Abner W. Colgate, Mr. and Mrs. Samuel J. Colgate, William Coleman, Mr. and Mrs. Hugh Ling Cole, Mrs. Henry A. Cort, Mr. C. Livingston Clarkson, and Miss Margaret Livingston Clarkson.

D.

Mr. and Mrs. Coleman Drayton, Mr. and Mrs. De Forest, Miss Duer, Mr. and Mrs. Delafield, Miss Delafield, Mr. and Mrs. Edward Tiffany Dyer, Mark De Wolf, Mr. and Mrs. Harvey Durand, Mr. and Mrs. Benjamin F. Dunning, William Dules, Frank Drummond, the Misses

Dresser, James Douglas, Mr. and Mrs. J. Otto Donner, Miss Bessie Donner, Mr. and Mrs. Charles T. Dillingham, Mr. and Mrs. Wm. B. Dinsmore, Miss Helen Dinsmore, Mr. and Mr. C. Dickinson, Miss C. Dickinson, Eugene E. Dewey, Mr. and Mrs. George De Witt, Mr. and Mrs. Charles De Rham, Mr. and Mrs. John T. Denny, Mr. and Mrs. Jacob De Neufille, Mr. and Mrs. Francis Ogden De Luze, E. De Lima, Miss Frances Delprat, Mr. and Mrs. Warren Delano, of Orange, Mr. and Mrs. Franklin H. Delano, Mr. and Mrs. E. Ritzema De Grove, Mrs. Theodore Dehon, Miss M. H. Dehon, Mr. and Mrs. Daniel A. Davis, Judge and Mrs. John Davis, of Washington, Mr. and Mrs. Clarence Day, Mr. and Mrs. Alfred De Castro, Mr. and Mrs. Alfred De Cordova, George Lord Day, Miss Susan De Forest Day, Mr. and Mrs. George B. De Forest, Melville Day, Mr. and Mrs. William H. Davis, Mrs. B. F. Dawson, Mr. and Mrs. T. M. Davis, Mr. and Mrs. Paul Dana, Count and Countess Gaston d'Auschot, of Washington, Benjamin Dana, Mr. and Mrs. J. Alfred Davenport, George Trimble Davidson, Mr. and Mrs. Robert K. Davies, Mrs. Dahlgren, of Washington, Mrs. Paul Dahlgren, of Newport, ex-Judge and Mrs. Charles P. Daly.

E.

Dr. and Mrs. John Haven Emerson, Mr. and Mrs. Devereux Emmet, Miss M. C. Endicott, H.

C. Eno, James Eugene Ernst, Dr. and Mrs. Alfred Eli, Mrs. Herman LeRoy Emmet, Mr. and Mrs. John Erving, the Misses Erving, of Rye, N. Y., Mrs. M. G. Evans, Mr. and Mrs. Fred B. Estes, Leopold Eidlitz, Mrs. Richard Elmer, Mr. and Mrs. John S. Ellis, of Barton, N. Y., Mr. and Mrs. Frederick B. Elliott, Richard McCall Elliott, Mr. and Mrs. Edward Earle, Mr. and Mrs. J. Pierrepont Edwards, Mr. and Mrs. Alfred L. Edmonds, LeRoy Edgar, Frederick Edey, Mr. and Mrs. D. A. Easton, Mrs. Catherine Ellicott, William Struthers Ellis.

F.

Mr. and Mrs. Harris F. Fahnestock, Mrs. Adele A. Fabbricotti, Horace Fairbanks, Mr. and Mrs. H. R. Fairfax, Mr. and Mrs. Wm. H. Falconer, the Misses Falconer, Mrs. John M. Furman, the Misses Furman, Mr. and Mrs. Francis P. Furnald, Mr. and Mrs. Charles F. Frothingham, Mr. and Mrs. Horace W. Fuller, Seth Barton French, Miss French, Mr. and Mrs. Wilberforce Freeman, Mr. and Mrs. James B. Fry, Mr. and Mrs. Charles B. Foote, Mr. and Mrs. C. G. Francklyn, Mr. and Mrs. John Fox, Mr. and Mrs. D. Ogden Fowler, Frederick De Peyster Foster, Mr. and Mrs. Francis Forbes, James B. Ford, Mr. and Mrs. Wm. B. Foulke, Mr. and Mrs. John W. Fraley, Mr. and Mrs. Charles B. Fosdick, Col. De Lancey Floyd-Jones, Mr. and Mrs. Wm. G. Fleming, Mr.

and Mrs. Wm. Flagg, Mr. and Mrs. Wm. L. Findley, Mr. and Mrs. Hamilton Fish, Jr., Mr. and Mrs. Nicholas Fish, Mrs. Stuyvesant Fish, Mrs. Louis Fitzgerald, 'Miss Annie Flint, Theodore. Fitch, Mr. and Mrs. Wm. Baldwin Fitts, Mr. and Mrs. Cornelius Fellowes, Mr. and Mrs. Morris P. Ferris, the Misses Ferris, Miss Alice Field, Mr. and Mrs. Cortlandt De Peyster Field, Mr. and Mr. Henry A. Ferguson, Mr. and Mrs. Henry Fanshawe, of Norristown, N. J., Mrs. Edward A. Farrington, Mr. and Mrs. George R. Fearing, of Newport, Mr. and Mrs. John Farr. of Short Hills, N. J., Mr. and Mrs. Maunsell Bradhust Field, of Peekskill, N. Y., Percival Farquhar, Mr. and Mrs. W. Fanning.

G.

Miss Gallatin, Mr. and Mrs. Albert H. Gallatin, Mr. and Mrs. Frederick Gallatin, Mr. and Mrs. James Gallatin, Mr. and Mrs. William Gammell, Jr., of Newport, Mrs. James T. Gilbert, the Misses Gilbert, Mrs. Harry D. Gibson, Mr. and Mrs. Theodore Kane Gibbs, James Gaunt, Mr. and Mrs. George J. Gerr, John B. Gerrish, Bancroft Gherardi, Mr. and Mrs. Sheppard Gandy, George Austin Gardiner, Mr. and Mrs. Francis Garrettson, Col. and Mrs. Gardiner, Miss De Garmendia, Charles E. Gautier, Mr. and Mrs. Harrison E. Gawtry, Mr. and Mrs. C. H. Godfrey, Miss Edith Godfrey, Mr. and Mrs. Calvin Goddard, Miss

Hope Goddard, Miss Glover, Mr. and Mrs. John P. Gillis, Mr. and Mrs. William Gihon, Miss Jeanette L. Gilder, Miss Sally Gillet, Mr. and Mrs. Arthur Coit Gilman, R. Swain Gifford, Mr. and Mrs. Richard Gilder, Mr. and Mrs. Frederick Goodridge, the Misses Goodridge, Mr. and Mrs. James K. Gracie, Mr. and Mrs. Joseph Grafton, Miss Margaret M. Gouley, Mr. and Mrs. Almon Goodwin.

H.

Mr. and Mrs. S. S. Howland, Mr. and Mrs. J. G. Hecksher, the Hon. and Mrs. Herbert, Miss Hargous, Mr. and Mrs. Hillhouse, John Hyslop, Mr. and Mrs. Henry B. Hyde, Louis T. Hoyt, Miss H. F. Hubbard, Mr. and Mrs. Laurence Hutton, Mrs. S. J. Hurtt, the Misses Huntington, Charles Gordon Hutton, Mr. and Mrs. Clarence G. Hyde, the Misses Hunter, Mr. and Mrs. Thomas Hunter, Miss Hoyt, Mr. and Mrs. Charles Hubbell, Mrs. Susan E. Johnson-Hudson, the Misses Humbert, Mr. and Mrs. Arthur M. Hunter, Dr. and Mrs. George Humphreys, Mr. and Mrs. John M. Hughes, Sidney W. Hopkins, Mr. and Mrs. Wm. Warner Hoppin, Jr., Mr. and Mrs. Barett Wilson Horton, Miss May Hoyt, Miss Gertrude Hoyt, B. Hunting Howell, the Misses Howard, Miss Caroline Hopkins, Mrs. Hamilton Hoppin, Mr. and Mrs. James Buchanan Houston, Mr. and Mrs. George R. Howell, Mr. and Mrs.

Artemas H. Holmes, Mrs. Douglas Hollister, John Hone, Miss Margaret D. Hone, Mr. and Mrs. Archibald Hopkins, Roland Holt, Miss E. L. Holly, Mr. and Mrs. Charles Holt, Mr. and Mrs. Sheppard Homans, Mrs. A. Hollister, Miss Grace Holbrook, Mr. and Mrs. Henry L. Hoguet, Col. and Mrs. Wm. Hoffman, Miss Hoffman, Miss Susan Hoffman, Miss Isabel W. Hoffman, Bradford Hitchcock, Thomas Howard, Mr. and Mrs. S. A. Hodge, Jr., Mr. and Mrs. James J. Higginson, Mrs. Elias S. Higgins, the Misses Hewitt, Mr. and Mrs. Cooper Hewitt, Mr. and Mrs. John Herriman, Miss Emmie Hecksher, Miss Sarah H. Haswell, Miss Havemeyer, Mr. and Mrs. Horn.

I.

R. Livingston Ireland, the Misses Ireland, Cortlandt Irving, Mr. and Mrs. Adrian Iselin, Jr., the Misses Iselin, Isaac Iselin, Charles H. Isham, Miss Helen C. Irving, Miss Frances R. Irving, Mr. and Mrs. J. Bruce Ismay, Mr. and Mrs. W. B. Isham, Miss Helen Iselin, Mr. and Mrs. Brayton Ives.

J.

Mr. and Mrs. John Brinckerhoff Jackson, the Misses Jackson, John H. Jacquetin, Edgar M. Johnson, Miss Ethel Johnson, Mr. and Mrs. R. Dickinson Jewett, Mr. and Mrs. Charles Jesup, Mr. and Mrs. Wm. Travers Jerome, Mrs. Lawrence R. Jerome, Augustus E. Jesup, Mr. and Mrs. Augustus Jay, Col. and Mrs. Wm. Jay, Arthur Curtiss James, John G. Janeway, Miss Maud Jarvis, Miss Josephine Jarvis, Mrs. H. Le Roy Jones, Miss Mary Jones, Mrs. Wm. Francis Judson, Mr. and Mrs. Augustus D. Juilliard, Mrs. Lewis Colford Jones, Charles A. Joy.

K.

De Lancey Kane, Woodbury Kane, Mr. and Mrs. Greenville Kane, the Misses Kean, Mr. and Mrs. John James Key, Jr., Mr. and Mrs. Chauncey F. Kerr, Mr. and Mrs. James P. Kernochan, Mrs. John A. Kernochan, Mr. and Mrs. George W. Kid, Mrs. Archibald Gracie King, Miss Anna A. Knapp, Mr. and Mrs. Rudolph Herman Kissel, John Parish Kingsford, Mr. and Mrs. H. S. Kingsley, Col. and Mrs. Lawrence Kip, Miss Lawrence Kip, Miss Edith Kip, Mr. and Mrs. Ambrose Kingsland, Mr. and Mrs. Benjamin P. Kissam, Mr. and Mrs. Richard King, Jr., Mr. and Mrs. Edward Bronson King, Mr. and Mrs. Luther Kountze, Mr. and Mrs. Augustus Kountze, Gouverneur Kortright, Miss Keebe, Henry P. King, of Boston.

L.

Mr. and Mrs. Richard Lounsbery, Mr. and Mrs. Grosvenor P. Lowrey, Mr. and Mrs. Charles Lyman, Mr. and Mrs. E. Livingston Ludlow, Mr.

and Mrs. E. McEvers Livingston, of Lenox, Mrs. Maturin Livingston, the Misses Livington, Mr. and Mrs. Wm. S. Livingston, Jr., Mr. and Mrs. Pierre Lorillard, Mr. and Mrs. Louis Lorillard, Miss F. B. Lockwood, Frank Loomis, Mrs. Annette W. W. Hicks-Lord, Mr. and Mrs. George De Forest Lord, Mr. and Mrs. Joseph H. Locke, Miss Locke, Johnston Livingston, Miss Livingston, Mr. and Mrs. Raymond Lesher, Mr. and Mrs. Edward LeRoy, Mr. and Mrs. Newbold LeRoy, the Misses Lintilhon, Mr. and Mrs Levi Leiter, Miss Leiter, Mr. and Mrs. Benjamin Franklin Lee, Mr. and Mrs. J. Bowers Lee, the Misses Lee, Mr. and Mrs. Newbold T. Lawrence, Mr. and Mrs. Prescot Lawrence, Mr. and Mrs. Edward La Montagne, the Misses La Montagne.

M.

Mr. and Mrs. R. Mortimer, Mr. and Mrs. Clarence McKim, Miss McKim, Peter Marie, Miss Leotine Marie, Miss Josephine Marie, Mr. and Mrs. Charles V. Mapes, Mr. and Mrs. Frank Halsey Man, Mr. and Mrs. George C. Magoun, Mr. and Mrs. Thomas A. Maitland, Charles W. Maury, the Misses Mason, Mr. and Mrs. Henry Marquand, Miss Mabel Marquand, Henry M. Marquand, Chauncey H. Marshall, Howard Townsend Martin, James Milliken, Miss N. D. B. Miller, the Misses Miller, Mr. and Mrs. Alphonse Montant,

Jules A. Montant, Mr. and Mrs. J. Pierpont Morgan, the Misses Morgan, Mr. and Mrs. James Mortimer Montgomery, Miss Katherine Montague, Mr. and Mrs. John Chandler Moore, Mr. and Mrs. Wm. Gouverneur Morris, Miss Morris, Mr. and Mrs. George Austin Morrison, D. Herman Morris, Mr. and Mrs. Jose M. Munoz, Mrs. Jordan L. Mott, Mr. and Mrs. Lewis Champlin Murdock, Wm. Bronson Murry, Percy Musgrave, Mrs. L. B. Musgrave, J. Archibald Murray, R. L. W. Moss, Mr. and Mrs. Sidney Morse, C. Austin Meigs, Wm. S. Mayo.

N.

The Misses Nash, Alphonso De Navarro, Mr. and Mrs. D. John Means, Mrs. Wm. Neilson, Mr. and Mrs. Frederick R. Newbold, of Newport, Mr. and Mrs. Francis G. Newlands, Mr. and Mrs. George S. Nicholas, Mrs. Wm. Curtis Noyes, Mrs. L. J. De W. Clarkson Nunn, Oliver H. Northcote, the Misses Norris, Mr. and Mrs. Gordon Norrie, Wm. B. Northrup.

O.

Mr. and Mrs. Otis, Miss Otis, Adolph E. Outerbridge, Mr. and Mrs. James W. Otis, Mr. and Mrs. W. H. Osgood, Miss Elizabeth A. Osgood, Mr. and Mrs. Wm. Oothout, J. Victor Onativia, Stephen Henry Olin, Miss Mary S. Ogden, Mr. and Mrs. Ludlow Ogden.

P.

Mr. and Mrs. Howland Pell, Mr. and Mrs. C. L. Perkins, Miss Perkins, Mr. and Mrs. William Post, Mr. and Mrs. Henry Parish, the Misses Parish, Mr. and Mrs. Franklin A. Paddock, Mr. and Mrs. Trenor L. Park, Mr. and Mrs. Cortlandt Parker, the Misses Parker, James C. Parrish, Mr. and Mrs. Paton, Miss Paton, Wm. Parsons, Mr. and Mrs. John E. Parsons, Mr. and Mrs. Thomas L. Pearsall, Dr. and Mrs. George Livingston Peabody, Judge and Mrs. Chas. A Peabody, Gouverneur Paulding, of Cold Spring, N. Y., Miss Mary Peckham, Mr. and Mrs. Chas. Pelham Clinton, Frederick A. Pell, Mr. and Mrs. Herbert C. Pell, Henry Phelps, Mr. and Mrs. Samuel T. Peters, Mrs. Charles L. Perkins, Mr. and Mrs. James H. Percival, Mr. and Mrs. H. E. Pellew, of Washington, Mrs. Henry Pierrepont, the Misses Pierrepont, of Brooklyn, Mr. and Mrs. John Jay Phelps, Mr. and Mrs. Edward Potter, Miss Grace Potter, Mrs. Robert B. Potter, of Newport, Mr. and Mrs. Percy Pyne, Jr.

R.

Mr. and Mrs. J. R. Roosevelt, Mr. and Mrs. R. G. Remsen, Miss Remsen, Mr. and Mrs. Roland Redmond, Mr. and Mrs. Geraldyn Redmond, the Misses Rutherford, Mr. and Mrs. E. K. Rositer, Mr. and Mrs. James Roosevelt, Miss Anita

B. Roosevelt, Henry G. Russell, of Providence, Mr. and Mrs. Wm. H. Ross, the Misses Ross, Mrs. Hilborn Roosevilt, Reginald Ronalds, Miss Harriet Rogers, Mr. and Mrs. Wm. E. Rogers, Mr. and Mrs. F. M. Robeling, of Trenton, Mr. and Mrs. Fairman Rogers, of Philadelphia, Mrs. Beverly Robinson, Miss Genevieve Phelps Robbins, Miss Mary A. Robbins, Mr. and Mrs. Frederick Robert, David M. Ripley, Mr. and Mrs. Reginald W. Rives, C. Frederick Richards, Mr. and Mrs. Henry M. Requa, Wm. Remsen, Mr. and Mrs. Henry Redmond, Mr. and Mrs. J. Van D. Reed, Charles Renauld.

S.

Mrs. Robert Schuyler, Miss Schermerhorn, Mr. and Mrs. Wm. Schieffelin, Mr. and Mrs. S. S. Sands, Miss Sands, Mr. and Mrs. John Suydam, Mrs. Gerard Stuyvesant, of Newport, Rutherford Stuyvesant, Mr. and Mrs. Wm. E. Strong, Mrs. John A. Stoutenburgh, the Misses Stoutenburgh, Gustave Stromberg, Mr. and Mrs. Richard Collier St. John, Mr. and Mrs. Anson Phelps Stokes, Miss Stokes, Mr. and Mrs. Roy Stone, the Misses Stockton, of Trenton, Mr. and Mrs. Augustine St. Gaudens, John Austin Stevens, of Newport, the Misses Stevens, Mr. and Mrs. Henry D. Steers, Mrs. Ichabod P. Stephens, Robert Livingston Stevens, of Castle Point, Mr. and Mrs. Ed-

mund C. Stanton, Miss Betty Sperry, of Wilmington, Del., Mr. and Mrs. W. D. Sloane, Mr. and
Mrs. Wm. Winslow Sherman, Mrs. Elliott Shep-
ard, Mr. and Mrs. J. Egmont Schermerhorn.

T.

The Misses Turnure, L. Turnure, Mr. Travers,
the Misses Travers, Mr. and Mrs. Wm. Turnbull,
Mr. and Mrs. Alfred Tuckerman, Miss Lucy
Trowbridge, of New Haven, Reverdy Johnson
Travers, Mrs. Wm. R. Travers, Mr. and Mrs.
Wm. W. Tompkins, of Lenox, Mr. and Mrs. J.
Kennedy Tod, Joseph Thorow, of Washington,
Mr. and Mrs. James Thomson, Baron and Bar-
oness C. de Thomsen, Mr. and Mrs. Wm. H.
Tailer, Mr. and Mrs. Edward U. Tailer, the Misses
Tailer, Mrs. James Tyng.

V.

Miss Bessie Van Rensselaer, Mr. Eugene Van
Rensselaer and Miss Van Rensselaer, of Virginia,
James M. Varnum, the Misses Varnum, Stewart
Van Vliet, Mr. and Mrs. Cornelius D. Van Wag-
enen, Miss Helen E. Villard.

W.

Mr. and Mrs. E. R. Wharton, Mr. and Mrs.
Frank Wissman, Mr. and Mrs. Robert Winthrop,
Egerton Winthrop, Mr. and Mrs. J. C. Wilmer-

ding, Miss Wilmerding, Mr. and Mrs. Edward H.
Weatherbee, Mr. and Mrs. W. W. Watrous, Mr.
and Mrs. James M. Waterbury, Mr. and Mrs. Benjamin Wells, Miss Wells.

Y. and Z.

Fernando A. Yznaga, Mr. and Mrs. John A. Di
Zerega, Miss Chalotte Di Zerega, Mr. and Mrs.
Louis H. Di Zerega.

SOME OF THE COSTUMES.

Of the hundreds of beautiful costumes which
were worn, the more notable ones follow. There
were many imported gowns, principally from
Worth and Felix, but the New York dressmakers
showed by the exhibition of their workmanship
that they need fear no rivals on the other side of
the Atlantic.

A.

Miss Florence Ascher, of Boston, wore a gown
of white satin, dancing length, covered with white
tulle, embroidered with silver bees. Upon the
satin skirt, at the bottom, was a fringe of silver,
the effect through the latter draperies being very
dainty. The waist was cut low, and was decorated
with silver embroidery. The ornaments were
diamonds, set in silver, and pearls. She carried a
great bunch of Puritan roses.

Miss Madeline Anthon's costume was of silver-gray silk and tulle, profusely decorated with silver. The foot of the dress was trimmed with several rows of silver lace, while the bodice, which was decollete, was richly embroidered with silver thread. Miss Anthon carried roses and wore diamond ornaments.

Miss Cecelia Andrews wore a Worth gown, of dancing length, of lilac silk and tulle. The bodice, which was cut low, was trimmed with lilac-colored marabou feathers about the shoulders, while the tulle draperies of the skirt had a similar decoration. She wore amethysts and pearls.

B.

Mrs. Calvin S. Brice wore an elaborate gown. The train was long and full, and was of white satin, heavily brocaded with silver. The front was draped with white mousseline de soie, embroidered with silver threads, and edged with silver fringe. The bodice was decollete of the brocade, and was ornamented with silver. Jewels were rare diamonds and decorations of flowers.

Miss Georgiana L. Berryman's gown was of yellow. The long train was of yellow satin. The front and sides were of yellow tulle, ornamented with satin ribbons and flowers; decollete bodice of the yellow, trimmed with gold. Jewels of diamonds and topazes. Ornaments with flowers.

Miss Sadie Brookman, of Brooklyn, wore a costume of silver-gray satin. The skirt was made dancing length, and was covered with a single thickness of gray tulle, spangled with silver. The bodice was of the satin and tulle, made decollete. Jewels were of diamonds.

Miss Minnie Brookman, of Brooklyn, wore a gown of white satin, made dancing length. It was covered with white tulle, and was profusely trimmed with holly berries and leaves and red ribbons. The bodice was decollete of the satin tulle. Jewels were pearls. Floral ornaments.

Mrs. Josiah Belden's costume was of white. The long full train was of heavy white brocade, while the front and sides were of white crepe de chine, embroidered with white silk, and trimmed with white marabou feathers. The bodice was decollete, and was of the brocade, and trimmed with crepe de chine and feathers. Diamond and floral ornaments.

Miss Henrietta Burden wore a gown of apple-green silk, of dancing length. The draperies were of mousseline de soie of the same shade, across the fabric of which was delicately embroidered in gold thread a slender ivy vine. The bodice was decollete, and was decorated with ivy leaves of gold embroidery, the trimming of the mousseline de soie being caught up on the left shoulder by a jeweled ivy leaf. Her hair was confined by a fillet of golden ivy leaves, in each of which sparkled a diamond.

Miss L. Beach wore a costume of light-blue satin, with demi-train, which was covered with pale-blue tulle. The skirt was richly garnished tulle, the decoration being of tea roses. The waist was decollete of the tulle and satin, and trimmed with silver. She carried a big bunch of tea roses, and wore turquoises and diamond ornaments.

Miss Helen Bryce's gown was of white satin and tulle, with demi-train and decollete bodice. The garniture was of lilies of the valley. The ornaments were of diamonds.

Mrs. James A. Burden wore a Worth costume of white satin and crape. The front was of white crape, entirely covered with rows of silver fringe continuing to the top of the low-cut bodice. The train was of white tulle. Ornaments of diamonds.

Miss Beekman's gown was of delicate pink satin and mousseline de soie, which was exquisitely embroidered with silver vines bearing grapes. The bodice was cut low, and was of the embroidered mousseline de soie. The costume was further decorated by a garniture of pink lilacs and leaves. The ornaments were a necklace of pink pearls and diamonds.

Miss Boucher, of Washington, wore a dainty

dress of white silk and tulle, embroidered with tiny designs in gold, the general effect being an exceedingly rich one. Her bodice was profusely trimmed with gold. Her ornaments were diamonds.

C.

Mrs. Grover Cleveland's costume was of white silk, made with long train and a decollete bodice. The garniture was of flowers. Diamond ornaments.

Mrs. Lindley H. Chapin wore a gown of white satin and tulle. The skirt was made with a long, full train, and was covered with white tulle. The front and sides were ornamented with gold passementerie and white satin ribbons. Decollete bodice ornamented with gold. Ornaments were a profusion of diamonds and flowers.

Mrs. R. Fulton Cutting's costume was a long-trained white satin gown, covered with white tulle, and profusely ornamented with gold and white marabou feathers. The bodice was decollete, and was of satin covered with tulle. The bodice had a gold stomacher, and was finished about the shoulders with white marabou feathers. The ornaments were of diamonds and pearls.

Miss Rosina Caldecorn, of Richmond, Va., wore a dainty gown of brocaded silk in a delicate shade of rose-pink. The skirt was plaited, and was trimmed with garlands of tiny rosebuds.

The combination of the green of the leaves, and the delicate shade of the silk and buds, was particularly effective. A necklace of pearls and diamonds, and an aigrette of diamonds, were her only ornaments. The bodice was cut low, and was of the brocade.

Miss Edith Clift's costume was of old-rose silk, with demi-train and decollete bodice, covered with old-rose tulle. The garniture of the gown was of American Beauty roses. Ornaments of diamonds.

Miss Bessie Clift wore a gown of blush-pink satin, covered with tulle of the same color. The bodice was low-cut, and was of satin, covered with tulle. The costume was garnitured with blush-roses and rose leaves. Ornaments of pearls.

Mrs. William Bayard Cutting wore an Empire gown, the front of which was of white tulle, striped with gold, draped over white satin. It was finished across the foot with a deep fringe of lilacs and green leaves. The train was of white tulle. The bodice was decollete, and was of gold and white, with a garniture of lilacs. Ornaments of diamonds.

Mrs. Henry Clews' costume was of mauve-colored satin, covered with mauve-colored tulle, and trimmed with silver. The waist was decollete, and was of tulle. On each shoulder she wore an epaulet of pale-green velvet, spangled with silver. Her ornaments were the diamonds for which her toilets are famous.

Miss Catlin wore a gown of plush pink and white satin and mousseline de soie, the skirt and bodice being of pink, and the draperies being of the white semi-transparent material, which was profusely embroidered with silver roses. The bodice, which was decollete, was trimmed with silver, and was garnished with tiny rosebuds. Her ornaments were diamonds.

Miss Caswell's gown was a simple dress of dancing length, the skirt and bodice, which was decollete, being of white satin, trimmed with mousseline de soie of the same negative shade. Her ornaments were pearls.

Miss Ida Coster wore a costume of pale-blue silk and tulle, with demi-train. The bodice, which was cut low, was, with the skirt, elaborately garnitured with marguerites. Miss Coster wore a number of the same flowers in her hair. Her ornaments were sapphires and diamonds.

Mrs. MacGrane Coxe wore a gown of white brocade, the front of which, and the long train, was of the brocade. The left side was of alternate plaits of the brocade and plain white satin, the plain plaits being covered with real old white point lace, and ornamented with bunches of buttercup-color and white ostrich feathers. Down the

center of the back of the train, which was square,
was a band of white ostrich feathers. The bodice
of the brocade was decollete, and was trimmed
with lace and the buttercup-colored satin ribbons.
On the left shoulder was a bunch of buttercup-
colored and white ostrich feathers. Her ornaments
were of diamonds.

D.

Mrs. Frederick J. De Peyster wore a gown of
maize-colored moire. The train was of the moire,
and was very long and full. The front and sides
were draped with mousseline de soie of the same
color, and were trimmed with real white lace and
garlands of violets. The bodice was decollete of
the moire, and was trimmed with the mousseline
de soie and lace, and was edged about the shoulders with violets. The lace was caught on the
left shoulder with a large butterfly of emeralds.
The front of the waist was ornamented with five
large diamond stars. Mrs. De Peyster wore an
aigrette of diamonds in her hair, a necklace of
great stones, and the famous ear-rings.

Miss Florence Dalrymple wore a white silk
dress, made dancing length, covered with white
tulle, edged around the bottom with several rows
of white watered ribbon. The bodice was decollete, and was edged around the shoulders with
silver ornaments and lace. With this was worn

a broad white watered sash. Ornaments of pearls.

Mrs. Francis Delafield's costume was of old rose; the train was long, and was of old rose satin, brocaded with daffodils in their natural colors. The front and sides were of plain old rose satin, draped with old Venetian point lace. The bodice was decollete, with a garniture of pink ostrich feathers. Ornaments of diamonds.

Mrs. Henry Du Pont, of Wilmington, Del., wore a gown, the petticoat of which was of white satin, brocaded with yellow buttercups. The corset, train, and low-cut bodice were of golden brown velvet, edged with lynx tails. The stomacher of the bodice was of gold. Ornaments were of diamonds, rubies, and blush roses.

E.

Miss Laura Edwards wore a costume, the front and sides of which were of pink satin, draped with old cream-colored lace. The long, full train was of olive velvet, and where the train and sides joined were broad bands of pink ostrich feathers. The bodice was decollete, and was of the velvet. The vest was of pink, draped with the lace, and the bodice was finished about the neck with pink marabou feathers.

Miss Eaton's costume was of light-green silk, covered with pale-green tulle spangled with silver. Tabliers at the sides were of cloth of silver. The decollete bodice was of cloth of silver, and the garniture was of pink rosebuds. Ornaments of diamonds and emeralds.

Mrs. James A. Edgar wore a dress, the long, full train and bodice of which were of black satin, brocaded with pink apple blossoms. The front and sides of the skirt were draped with old pink crepe de chine and deep silk fringe of the same shade. The front of the bodice was draped with the crepe de chine. The garniture was of pink ostrich tips and flowers.

F.

Mrs. Sigourney Fay's costume was of gray. The petticoat was of white satin brocade, the design of the brocade being carried out in hand embroidery and silver. Over this, in front, fell a broad tablier of silver-gray satin brocade, embroidered about the edge to match the petticoat. The train was long and full, of the gray brocade, with same embroidery as the rest of the costume. The bodice was decollete, and was of the gray brocade, with a stomacher of silver, and was finished about the shoulders with white marabou feathers. Ornaments of diamonds.

Miss Floyd-Jones' costume was of a salmon-colored brocade, the front being of white satin, embroidered with gold, and edged at the sides with white and salmon-colored marabou feathers.

The train and the decollete bodice were of the salmon-colored brocade. The garniture of the bodice was gold lace and pink and white feathers. Diamond and floral ornaments.

G.

Mrs. James W. Gerard's costume was of white satin, brocaded with silver. The train was long and full, of the silver brocade. The front and sides were of a combination of yellow satin brocade and apple-green velvet. The bodice was decollete, and was of the green velvet, ornamented with silver. Mrs. Gerard wore a great number of diamonds and emeralds.

Miss Charlotte Goodridge wore a gown of white silk, made demi-train, covered with white tulle, and garnished with white lilacs and green leaves. The bodice was decollete, and was edged about the neck and sleeves with white lilacs. The ornaments were of pearls and diamonds.

Miss Caroline Goodridge's costume was of pale-pink silk, made demi-train and decollete, and was covered with pale-pink tulle. The garniture was profuse, and was of a tiny pink flower. Ornaments of pearls.

Mrs. G. Griswold wore an imported gown, the front of which was of mousseline de soie, with embroidery of gold running to the top of the decollete bodice. The long court train was of white satin, brocaded with yellow velvet flowers. The costume was garnished with yellow roses and ivy leaves. The bodice was of the brocade. The ornaments were of diamonds.

Miss Emma Garson, of San Francisco, wore a Josephine gown of dandelion-colored bengaline, with panels of white mousseline de soie embroidered with gold. A broad sash of the gold embroidered mousseline de soie was worn just below the bust, and tied in a large bow in the back. Ornaments of pearls.

H.

Miss Sallie Hargous wore a pale-pink silk costume, with demi-train, covered with pale-pink tulle. The bodice was cut low. The garniture of the skirt and waist was of maiden-hair ferns. Her ornaments were diamonds and emeralds.

Mrs. A. E. Hazard wore a pink satin gown, the front of which was of the pink satin, trimmed with silver and clusters of pink roses. The train and the decollete bodice were of the pink tulle, the latter being trimmed with silver and a garniture of pink roses. The ornaments were diamonds.

I.

Mrs. Columbus O'D. Iselin's gown was copied after that of a figure in a painting in Versailles. It was of the sixteenth century. It was made of white pompadour brocade, real white lace; and a profufusion of gold ornamentation. Her ornaments were her magnificent diamonds.

Miss Winifred Ives wore a costume, the train of which was of white tulle, spangled with silver. The front of the skirt was of white brocade. The bodice was of the white and silver tulle, cut decollete. Ornaments of pearls and flowers.

J.

Mrs. Henry Janin wore a costume of pale-pink satin, the skirt of which was made demi-train, and was covered with pale-pink tulle. The garniture was of pink roses, and rose leaves and pink ribbons. The bodice was decollete, and was of the pink satin, covered with tulle, and edged about the shoulders with rose leaves. She carried a bouquet of La France roses. Ornaments of diamonds.

L.

Mrs. Herbert Langdon, of Boston, wore a costume of pale-pink satin, covered with pale-pink tulle, over which were rose leaves, fastened with crystal beads. The dress was made dancing length, the bodice cut decollete, and ornamented with pale-pink roses. Jewels of diamonds and pink pearls.

Mrs. Robert Henry L. Latham, of Philadelphia, had a gown of black satin, covered with black tulle, made *en traine*. The bodice was cut decollete, with a stomacher of gold. She wore black kid gloves and a necklace of great diamonds. Floral ornaments.

Mrs. Charles Lanier's costume was of pale-pink satin, covered with pale-pink tulle. The bodice was decollete, and both skirt and bodice were garnitured with pink and white lilacs. Ornaments of diamonds.

M.

Mrs. A. Newbold Morris wore a gown of black and gold. The train was long and full, of black satin, covered with black tulle. The front and sides were of black satin, with yellow satin let in, and were covered with real lace. The bodice was decollete of the satin and tulle, and was ornamented with gold. Diamond ornaments.

Miss Juliet Morris' costume was of white satin, covered with satin tulle. The front at the bottom was edged with a heavy, deep fringe of pale-pink roses. The decollete bodice was finished about the shoulders with pale-pink roses. Ornaments of diamonds.

Mrs. Robert Mesereau, of Baltimore, wore a costume which was particularly noteworthy. The long, full train was of pale amethyst-colored velvet. The front and sides were of white satin, covered and draped with white mousseline de soie, elegantly embroidered with silver, gold, and seed pearls. The bodice was decollete of the velvet, the front being trimmed with the mousseline de soie, caught on the left shoulder with white ostrich tips. Her necklace was a very beautiful one, of pale amethysts, surrounded with diamonds.

Miss Eva Morris' gown was of pale-green satin, made demi-train, with decollete bodice. The skirt and bodice were profusely decorated with brier roses. Her ornaments were some very beautiful family emeralds and diamonds.

Miss Annie Murray wore a costume of heliotrope silk, covered with heliotrope tulle, made demi-train and decollete, and trimmed with silver. The ornaments were of diamonds and flowers.

N.

Mrs. H. Victor Newcomb's gown was of yellow satin, covered with yellow tulle, and made with a long, full train. It was elaborately decorated with black silk poppies. The bodice was decollete, and was bordered about the shoulders with black poppies. The jewels were diamonds.

P.

Mrs. Arthur Paget's gown was of white and gold. The train was long and full, of gold-colored satin. The front and sides of the skirt were in large box-plaits of white satin, heavily brocaded with gold thread. Between the plaits were strips of the gold-colored satin, covered with a fringe of gold and amber beads. The bodice, decollete, was edged with marabou feathers, and was of the gold-colored satin, with a narrow vest of the brocade. Ornaments, diamonds.

Mrs. Henry Post wore a costume which was of rich gray brocade. The train was very long and full, and was, with the skirt, trimmed with a deep flounce of black thread lace. The bodice was cut with square neck and with three-quarter sleeves. It was trimmed with the lace. Ornaments were a remarkably brilliant display of diamonds.

Miss Nathalie Post's gown was very simple, being a white silk dress with demi-train, covered with white tulle. The garniture was of small white flowers. The ornaments were of pearls.

Miss Spriggie Post wore a yellow satin dress covered with tulle. The front of the dress was of the satin, with festoons of gold. The demi-train and decollete bodice were of the yellow tulle. Her costume was garnished with flowers. Diamond ornaments.

R.

Mrs. Edward H. Ripley's costume was very beautiful. The train was of blue satin, brocaded with buttercups. The front and sides were of yellow and blue changeable silk, and were draped with crepe de chine of the same shades. The bodice was low-cut, and was of the brocade, trimmed with the crepe de chine, and edged with marabou feathers. The ornaments were diamonds and sapphires.

Mrs. Henry Ascher Robbins wore a gown of black and pink. The front and sides were of pink pompadour brocade, with oak leaves embroidered in silver sequins. Across the foot of the front and sides was a ruching of crushed roses. At the left side was a panel of velvet autumn leaves and large silver apples. The train was covered with black tulle; the waist of black satin and pink velvet, and was cut decollete. Ornaments of flowers and diamonds.

Miss Bessie Rogers wore a white silk dress, the front and sides of which were entirely covered with tulle, ornamented with bachelor buttons. The demi-train was of plain white tulle. The bodice was decollete, and was of the white tulle, ornamented with the bachelor buttons. Fastened at either shoulder were knots of bright red velvet, which continued down the back in broad sashes to the end of the train. Ornaments of diamonds and rubies.

Miss Robins' gown was of white and silver tulle, the front and sides of which were of pale-green satin, festooned with tiny pink rosebuds, pink ribbons, and maiden-hair ferns. The train and decollete bodice were of the silver spangled tulle, the latter having a garniture of rosebuds. The ornaments were of emeralds and pearls,

Her head-dress was of rosebuds and the maiden-hair ferns.

S.

Mrs. Sharon, of San Francisco, wore a dress, made dancing length, the skirt being of pale-green silk, the back of which was covered with green tulle, spangled with gold. The front and sides were of puffs of pale-green tulle, held in place by perpendicular bands of heavy gold passementerie. The bodice was decollete of the silk, covered with plain tulle, with a stomacher of gold, and was edged about the shoulders with pale-pink marabou feathers. The ornaments were diamonds and emeralds.

Miss Madeline Le Roy Satterlee's gown was of white satin, with demi-train, and was covered with white tulle. It was profusely trimmed with yellow ribbons and white violets. The bodice was decollete, and trimmed about the shoulders with white violets. Ornaments of diamonds and pearls.

T.

Mrs. J. B. Travers' costume was of mauve and white, the train being full of the mauve satin. The front and sides were of white satin, with pointed gold ornaments beginning wide at the bottom and running half way to the waist-line. At the sides were broad bands of white marabou feathers. The bodice was cut decollete of mauve satin, trimmed with gold and marabou feathers. The gems were diamonds, topazes, and pearls.

Mrs. Herbert L. Terrell wore a gown with a princess back of white brocade, the train being very long and full. The front and sides were of white satin, edged with deep white silk fringe. The waist was of white mousseline de soie, and was caught up on the left shoulder with a knot of the fringe and a bunch of white ostrich tips. It was cut decollete. Ornaments were of diamonds and pearls.

Mrs. Hamilton McK. Twombly wore an Empire gown of white and gold. The front was embroidered with threads of gold metal on the white ground. One side of the costume was of primrose-colored satin, and the other was of white mousseline de soie, embroidered with golden threads, and held in place by bands of real gold lace. The train was of white satin, and the bodice was decollete, of white satin, trimmed with the embroidered mousseline de soie. Mrs. Twombly wore most of her famous collection of diamonds.

V.

Mrs. Cornelius Vanderbilt wore an imported gown of light brocade, long, full train, and bodice decollete. The costume was profusely ornamented with jewels.

Mrs. Van Doren wore a gown of silver-gray

satin, brocaded with silver. The train was long and full of the brocade, while the front and sides had a deep flounce of black thread lace set in. The bodice was of the brocade, cut low. The ornaments were particularly large and beautiful diamonds.

Miss Van Nest's costume was of white satin and tulle, with demi-train. The front of the skirt was of the tulle, spangled with silver beads, while the train was plain. The bodice, which was decollete, and the skirt, were garnished with lilies of the valley. Ornaments of diamonds.

Mrs. Alexander Van Rensselear, wore a white dress of satin brocade, the design of the brocade being of lavender velvet rose leaves. The train was long and full, and was of the brocade, partly draped with lavender-colored mousseline de soie. The bodice was cut low, and was of the brocade and the mousseline de soie. Ornaments were of diamonds.

Miss Mabel Van Rensselear wore a simple costume of white silk, with demi-train, and covered with tulle. The bodice was cut low, and it and the skirt were garnished with pink lilacs. Her ornaments were pearls.

W.

Mrs. Wm. C. Whitney's gown was of yellow ottoman silk. The front was of the silk, and down either side, and across the bottom, were two broad bands of real gold lace. The demi-train was covered with yellow tulle, spangled with gold, held in place by knots of blue satin ribbon. The bodice was decollete, and was of the silk, trimmed with the lace. A sash of the satin ribbon was on the back. The costume was heavily garnitured with blue bachelor buttons. Her necklace was of sapphires and diamonds. In her hair Mrs. Whitney wore jeweled ornaments and an aigrette of yellow ostrich feathers.

Mrs. Walter Watson's costume was of white satin of notable richness, brocaded with a very large flower of black velvet. The front was of white crepe de chine, exquisitely embroidered with silver and mother-of-pearl. The bodice was decollete, and was of the brocade, trimmed with crepe de chine. Ornaments were of diamonds and flowers.

Mrs. S. V. White wore a gown of white brocade, which bore a figure more than a foot in length, making the train particularly noticeable, because of its heaviness and beauty. The front and sides were composed of a deep flounce of white crepe de chine, exquisitely embroidered with silver. The bodice was cut low, and was trimmed with the crepe de chine. The jewels were from Mrs. White's collection of diamonds.

Mrs. Charles Whittier's costume was of white

satin, demi-train, covered with white tulle, which was studded completely with white violets. The bodice was cut low, and was edged with the white violets. Ornaments of pearls.

Mrs. John J. Wysong wore a simple costume of white silk, covered with white tulle, spangled with silver. The bodice was decollete. The garniture of the costume was of pink roses. Diamond ornaments.

Mrs. W. Storrs Well's dress was of mauve-colored satin, covered with mauve-colored tulle. The bodice was decollete, and was garnitured with flowers. The ornaments were of topazes and diamonds.

Mrs. Alfred Wagstaff wore a gown of pale-pink brocade and tulle. The front and sides were of the brocade, trimmed with gold lace. The train and bodice were of the tulle, and the latter was trimmed with the gold lace. Her ornaments were of diamonds and pearls.

Mrs. Orme Wilson's gown was of yellow satin, covered with yellow tulle spangled with silver. The left side of the skirt was composed of alternate rows of silver embroidery, and white morning glories and green leaves. The bodice was decollete, and was garnitured with the morning glories. Diamond ornaments.

Y.

Mrs. Alfred Young's gown was of Nile-green

satin. The front and one side was of the green satin. The left side was of cloth of silver, so finished that it reflected like a mirror. Down each side of the panel were heavy bands of violets, which were reflected in the cloth of silver. The train was covered with silver-spangled tulle. The waist was of the green satin, trimmed with silver lace and the cloth of silver and violets. On each shoulder was an Alsacian knot of broad violet-colored ribbon, the ends of which were brought down and allowed to extend the full length of the train. Diamond and emerald ornaments.

WHY ENGLISH NOBLEMEN SEEK AMERICAN BRIDES.

Chauncey M. Depew's Views on the Subject.

"Why do Englishmen select American wives?" was asked the silver-tongued orator, Mr. Chauncey M. Depew, who submitted himself graciously to a reporter's inquisition on the subject of paramount interest and continuous discussion since the Endicott-Chamberlain wedding.

"Do you think I can answer that question without getting up another war with England? If I may express my opinion, without shattering the international treaty, I should say that the American girl has the advantage of her English sister in that she possesses all that the other lacks. This is due to the different methods in which the two girls are brought up. An English girl is, as a rule, brought up very strictly, kept under rigid discipline, sees nothing of society until formally brought out, is not permitted to think or act for

253

herself, or allowed to display any individuality. As a result she is shy, self-conscious, easily embarrassed, has little or no conversation, and needs to be helped, lifted. The English young man has not the helpful qualities that characterize the typical American masher, and, in consequence, the two present, as I have often seen them, a very helpless combination. Then the American girl comes along, prettier than her English sister, full of dash, and snap, and go, sprightly, dazzling, and audacious, and she is a revelation to the Englishman. She gives him more pleasure in one hour, at a dinner or ball, than he thought the universe could produce in a whole life-time. Speedily he comes to the conclusion that he must marry her or die. As a rule he belongs to an old and historic family, is well educated, traveled, and polished, but poor. He knows nothing of business, and to support his estate requires an increased income. The American girl whom he gets acquainted with has that income, so in marrying her he goes to heaven and gets—the earth."

"Which are best educated, American or English girls?"

"The English society girl is much better educated than the American, for the latter is rushed through the hotbed system of some stylish boarding school to be launched upon the social sea as a bud at sixteen, while the former is not only kept at school much longer, and taught more thoroughly, but in the quiet of country homes she educates herself, or, rather, is educated by the conversation about her in English politics, the characteristics of the party leaders on both sides, and the arguments for and against all measures agitating public opinion. She becomes bright, and suggestive, and alert as she grows older, and able to converse with men intelligently on all vital questions. Our conversation here is not thoughtful, profound, or argumentative; it is but the contact of the moment, a dinner, a reception, or a call, and we separate. Then they visit often for four months at the same country house, meet the same people, live intimately together, and conversation becomes discussion of serious and weighty considerations. The English married ladies are like our American girls, only they never get the spring and dash, quickness of repartee and chaff that our girls have, but they are the brightest and most venomous politicians in English society. Their houses are frequently political centers from which emanate influences that govern the nation. Our graduates of Wellesley, Vassar, Wells' College, and similar institutions, are the best educated women in the world; but a London lady said to me, 'They never come over here. We never see them.'"

"What do the English women say to the

American girls carrying off all their matrimonial prizes?"

"They criticise our girls very sharply for thus invading their domain, and attribute their success entirely to their fortunes. An English girl rarely has money, for either the estates are entailed upon the eldest sons, or the money is divided between the brothers, leaving the daughters with only a small allowance, while our girls share equally with their brothers. An Englishman worth $500,-000 gives his daughters $25,000 on marriage, and is called very generous, while an American father, worth the same amount, would think $100,000 none too much to bestow upon his daughter. An Englishman of the best class is not educated to business, and doesn't know how to earn a living in any way; besides there is no chance for a man in England, no good opening, and it is doubtless true that the large fortune the American girl possesses, or will inherit, does add to her attractiveness. English women claim that American girls have wonderful brilliancy and sparkle for the fashionable season, but that when thrown on their own resources in country houses, where serious discussion is the rule, they are found decidedly wanting, and know nothing of history, science, literature, politics, or religion."

"Are American girls received in the best society, and do they make no awkward mistakes?"

"Yes, they are received, and are very popular. London is the most hospitable city in the world. In its cosmopolitan society, composed of representatives from all nations, American girls bear off the palm; and as for mistakes, she avoids them with her ready tact and marvelous adaptability, which are her chief characteristics. There are few more successful and brilliant women in London than Lady Mandeville (Miss Consuella Yznaga), Mrs. Col. Paget, formerly Miss Minnie Stevens, called one of the handsomest women in society, and the Duchess of Marlborough, who in less than one month won her way to the front ranks, all of whom are New York girls; and Lady Churchill is one of the greatest political and social powers of Great Britain."

"Is more expected of English wives than of ours, and are American girls happy under the new restraints?"

"Nothing more is really expected of them socially; but an American girl sees that she must inform herself thoroughly on a variety of subjects unfamiliar to her, in order to compete with her capable English rivals, after the first two or three years, when the brilliancy and audacity so charming in a girl loses its novelty, or she will be looked upon as a butterfly imported with the radiance of her plumage diminishing year by year. She works hard at first, but she does enjoy the constant variety of her life. The year begins with the brilliant London season, with its perpetual series of royal receptions, balls, dinners, and teas, meeting the most illustrious and distinguished people in the world; then the yachting season, the shooting season, with all its excitements; the liberal hospitality of the country house, with its innumerable visitors representing every department of intellectual activity; the home, with its responsibilities; the parish work, tenants on the estate, children's schools, &c. ; and winds up with the Riviera and Rome before the season opens again."

"Which make the best wives, the American or English girls ?"

"Thank you—no; we don't commit ourselves on that subject."

THIS WONDERFUL MEDICINE

FOR

BILIOUS AND NERVOUS DISORDERS

is the most marvellous Antidote yet discovered. It is the premier Specific for Sick Headache and Indigestion ; and is found efficacious and remedial by **female sufferers.**

BEECHAM'S PILLS ACT LIKE MAGIC ON A WEAK STOMACH, and are the great Cure for SICK HEADACHE, IMPAIRED DIGESTION, CONSTIPATION, DISORDERED LIVER, etc.

Sold by all Druggists. Price, 25 cents per box. Prepared only by THOS. BEECHAM, St. Helens, Lancashire, England. B. F. ALLEN & CO., Sole Agents for the United States, 365 and 367 Canal Street, New York, who (if your druggist does not keep them) will mail **Beecham's Pills** on receipt of price—but inquire first. (Please mention TITLED AMERICANS.)

DENMAN THOMPSON'S OLD HOMESTEAD.

STREET & SMITH'S SELECT SERIES No. 23.

Price, 25 Cents.

Some Opinions of the Press.

"As the probabilities are remote of the play 'The Old Homestead' being seen anywhere but in large cities it is only fair that the story of the piece should be printed. Like most stories written from plays it contains a great deal which is not said or done on the boards, yet it is no more verbose than such a story should be, and it gives some good pictures of the scenes and people who for a year or more have been delighting thousands nightly. Uncle Josh, Aunt Tildy, Old Cy Prime, Reuben, the mythical Bill Jones, the sheriff and all the other characters are here, beside some new ones. It is to be hoped that the book will make a large sale, not only on its merits, but that other play owners may feel encouraged to let their works be read by the many thousands who cannot hope to see them on the stage."—*N. Y. Herald*, June 2d.

"Denman Thompson's 'The Old Homestead' is a story of clouds and sunshine alternating over a venerated home; of a grand old man, honest and blunt, who loves his honor as he loves his life, yet suffers the agony of the condemned in learning of the deplorable conduct of a wayward son; a story of country life, love and jealousy, without an impure thought, and with the healthy flavor of the fields in every chapter. It is founded on Denman Thompson's drama of 'The Old Homestead.'"—*N. Y. Press*, May 26th.

"Messrs. Street & Smith, publishers of the *New York Weekly*, have brought out in book-form the story of 'The Old Homestead,' the play which, as produced by Mr. Denman Thompson, has met with such wondrous success. It will probably have a great sale, thus justifying the foresight of the publishers in giving the drama this permanent fiction form."—*N. Y. Morning Journal*, June 2d.

"The popularity of Denman Thompson's play of 'The Old Homestead' has encouraged Street & Smith, evidently with his permission, to publish a good-sized novel with the same title, set in the same scenes and including the same characters and more too. The book is a fair match for the play in the simple good taste and real ability with which it is written. The publishers are Street & Smith, and they have gotten the volume up in cheap popular form."—*N. Y. Graphic*, May 29.

"Denman Thompson's play, 'The Old Homestead,' is familiar, at least by reputation, to every play-goer in the country. Its truth to nature and its simple pathos have been admirably preserved in this story, which is founded upon it and follows its incidents closely. The requirements of the stage make the action a little hurried at times, but the scenes described are brought before the mind's eye with remarkable vividness, and the portrayal of life in the little New England town is almost perfect. Those who have never seen the play can get an excellent idea of what it is like from the book. Both are free from sentimentality and sensation, and are remarkably healthy in tone."—*Albany Express*.

"Denman Thompson's 'Old Homestead' has been put into story-form and is issued by Street & Smith. The story will somewhat explain to those who have not seen it the great popularity of the play."—*Brooklyn Times*, June 8th.

"The fame of Denman Thompson's play, 'Old Homestead,' is world-wide. Tens of thousands have enjoyed it, and frequently recall the pure, lively pleasure they took in its representation. This is the story told in narrative form as well as it was told on the stage, and will be a treat to all, whether they have seen the play or not."—*National Tribune*, Washington, D. C.

"Here we have the shaded lanes, the dusty roads, the hilly pastures, the peaked roofs, the school-house, and the familiar faces of dear old Swanzey, and the story which, dramatized, has packed the largest theater in New York, and has been a success everywhere because of its true and sympathetic touches of nature. All the incidents which have held audiences spell-bound are here recorded—the accusation of robbery directed against the innocent boy, his shame, and leaving home; the dear old Aunt Tilda, who has been courted for thirty years by the mendacious Cy Prime, who has never had the courage to propose; the fall of the country boy into the temptations of city life, and his recovery by the good old man who braves the metropolis to find him. The story embodies all that the play tells, and all that it suggests as well."—*Kansas City Journal*, May 27th.

THE COUNTY FAIR.

By NEIL BURGESS.

Written from the celebrated play now running its second continuous season in New York, and booked to run a third season in the same theater.

The scenes are among the New Hampshire hills, and picture the bright side of country life. The story is full of amusing events and happy incidents, something after the style of our "Old Homestead," which is having such an enormous sale.

"**THE COUNTY FAIR**" will be one of the great hits of the season, and should you fail to secure a copy you will miss a literary treat. It is a spirited romance of town and country, and a faithful reproduction of the drama, with the same unique characters, the same graphic scenes, but with the narrative more artistically rounded, and completed than than was possible in the brief limits of a dramatic representation. This touching story effectively demonstrates that it is possible to produce a novel which is at once wholesome and interesting in every part, without the introduction of an impure thought or suggestion. Read the following

OPINIONS OF THE PRESS:

Any person who can laugh as heartily as did the big audience at the "County Fair" last evening will always enjoy good digestion.—*N. Y. Herald.*

Neil Burgess in the "County Fair" has never done anything better than the gentle-hearted New England spinster, and is worthy of commendation. —*N. Y. World.*

There are many amusing lines and situations in the "County Fair."— *N. Y. Tribune.*

In Neil Burgess' "County Fair" reproduction there is a great deal of pictorial truthfulness.—*N. Y. Sun.*

Words have been exhausted in praise of this admirable dramatic story of country life "down East."—*N. Y. News.*

Neil Burgess as Miss Abigail Prue in the "County Fair" took a firm hold from the start.—*N. Y. Times.*

The "County Fair" audience is not taken away from the country, and from the first introduction to Rock Bottom farm to the race at the county fair the scenes are rural.—*N. Y. Journal.*

"County Fair" touches the various chords of simple pathos and wholesome humor.—*N. Y. Press.*

Neil Burgess as Abigail Prue has forgotten none of those quaint mannerisms which have gained him fame as an impersonator of rustic female characters.—*N. Y. Telegram.*

From first to last he tickles the risibilities and appeals to the sympathies.—*N. Y. Commercial Advertiser.*

The County Fair is No. 33 of "The Select Series," for sale by all Newsdealers, or will be sent, on receipt of price, 25 cents, to any address, postpaid, by STREET & SMITH, Publishers, 25-31 Rose st., N. Y.

ANOTHER MAN'S WIFE.

An Entrancing Emotional Story,

By BERTHA M. CLAY.

No. I of the Primrose Edition of Copyright Novels.

Cloth. Price, $1.

SOME OPINIONS OF THE PRESS.

Messrs. Street & Smith, New York, begin a new series of novels—"The Primrose Library"—with "Another Man's Wife," by Bertha M. Clay. The story has enough plot to keep one from falling asleep over it, and it also indicates the stumbling-blocks and pitfalls which abound everywhere for young husbands and wives who think so much about having "a good time" that they have no time left in which to think about reputation and character.—*N. Y. Herald,* Sept. 10.

Street & Smith publish the American copyright novel, "Another Man's Wife," by Bertha M. Clay. It deals with certain corrupting influences of fashionable society, and impressively warns of the dangers that spring from them. Its plot is strong and dramatic, and is elaborated with all of the qualities of style that have made the author so popular. It is the first issue of the new Primrose Series.—*Boston Globe,* Sept. 16.

"Another Man's Wife," by Bertha M. Clay, Street & Smith's Primrose Series, is a laudable effort toward the repression of the growing evil of matrimonial disloyalty. The book is handsomely bound, with a holiday look about it.—*Brooklyn Eagle,* Sept. 15.

Street & Smith of New York publish in cloth cover "Another Man's Wife," by Bertha M. Clay. The story is effective. It impressively depicts the results certain to attend the sins of deception. It teaches a lesson that will not be lost upon those thoughtless men and women who, only intent upon pleasure, little dream of the pitfall before them, and to which they are blind until exposure wrecks happiness.—*Troy (N. Y.) Press.*

Street & Smith, New York, have brought out in book-form "Another Man's Wife." This is one of Bertha M. Clay's most effective stories.— *Cincinnati Enquirer.*

"Another Man's Wife." This is one of Bertha M. Clay's most effective stories. It forcibly and impressibly portrays the evils certain to attend matrimonial deceit, clandestine interviews, and all the tricks and devices which imperil a wife's honor. It has a novel and entrancingly interesting plot, and abounds in vivid and dramatic incidents. It is the first issue of Street & Smith's Primrose Edition of Copyright Novels, and will not appear elsewhere.—*Franklin Freeman.*

THE SELECT SERIES

OF

Popular American Copyright Stories,

BY NOTABLE AUTHORS.

NO. 15.

The Virginia Heiress

By MRS. MAY AGNES FLEMING,

AUTHOR OF

**"Guy Earlscourt's Wife," "A Wonderful Woman,"
"One Night's Mystery."**

A tame story has never come from the vigorous and versatile pen of May Agnes Fleming. "The Virginia Heiress" is a pleasantly written, yet powerful and life-like narrative of a flesh-and-blood heroine, who talks and acts as many self-willed beauties are inclined to talk and act. It is the short-lived romantic dream of a young woman of culture and refinement, accustomed to all the luxuries of wealth, whose mental vision at first does not range beyond the rose-colored haze of the honey-moon; but she at length descends from the clouds of the lovers' dreamland, with eyes wide open, and stares this startling fac: clearly in the face—she has married a poor man! He is not only poor—far worse than that; he is the associate of "men who dress for dinner by taking off their coats and dining in their shirt-sleeves."

PRICE, 25 CENTS.

STREET & SMITH, Publishers,

P. O. Box: 2734.   31 Rose Street, New York.

Published in Great Britain in 2013 by Old House books & maps,
c/o Osprey Publishing, PO Box 883, Oxford, OX1 9PL, UK
c/o Osprey Publishing, PO Box 3985, New York, NY 10185-3985, USA.
Website: www.oldhousebooks.co.uk

A CIP catalogue record for this book is available from the British
Library.

ISBN-13: 978 1 90840 260 8

Originally published in 1890 by Street & Smith, New York.
Printed in China through Worldprint Ltd.

13 14 15 16 17   10 9 8 7 6 5 4 3 2 1